PIVOT

Harit Nagpal is the CEO of Tata Play, India's largest content distribution platform. In a career spanning four decades, he has also worked with Lakmé, Marico, Pepsi, Shoppers Stop and Hutch/Vodafone. He has co-authored a case study on the subject of disruption, which is now a part of the curriculum at London Business School, and he teaches MBA students at NM College in Mumbai too. He is also the bestselling author of *Adapt: To Thrive, Not Survive.*

HARIT NAGPAL

PIVOT

Between two options,
pick the third

WESTLAND
BUSINESS

WESTLAND
BUSINESS

Published by Westland Business, an imprint of Westland Books, a division of Nasadiya Technologies Private Limited, in 2025

No. 269/2B, First Floor, 'Irai Arul', Vimalraj Street, Nethaji Nagar, Alapakkam Main Road, Maduravoyal, Chennai 600095

Westland, the Westland logo, Westland Business and the Westland Business logo are the trademarks of Nasadiya Technologies Private Limited, or its affiliates.

Copyright © Harit Nagpal, 2025

Harit Nagpal asserts the moral right to be identified as the author of this work.

ISBN: 9789371979092

10 9 8 7 6 5 4 3 2 1

The views and opinions expressed in this work are the author's own and the facts are as reported by him, and the publisher is in no way liable for the same.

All rights reserved

Typeset by Jojy Philip

Printed at Manipal Technologies Limited, Manipal

No part of this book may be reproduced, or stored in a retrieval system, or transmitted in any form or by any means, electronic, mechanical, photocopying, recording, or otherwise, without express written permission of the publisher.

CONTENTS

Introduction   vii

PART 1   What Do You Want to Be?   1

PART 2   What Will You Learn?   23

PART 3   What Will You Do?   53

PART 4   How Will You Stay at the Peak for Long?   119

INTRODUCTION

For most of my life, Neel has lived within me, and I've often seen him in others around me. However, I didn't give him much thought till I started writing *Pivot*.

Pivot helped me discover a pattern in how he grew up, what he studied, his work experiences and the kind of person all of this ultimately made him.

Neel started as an underconfident, shy and a passive kind of a boy like many children are. At some point, he started challenging traditions, albeit subconsciously. As his experience, confidence and safety net grew, his ability to look for an alternate path to follow or to prevent obsolescence became dominant elements of his persona. His favourite word, which he used often, became 'So?'. This would be his response to anyone who pointed out that he was deviating from the conventional path.

Neel would pivot as a habit, every day of his life, for decisions of consequence, even routine matters, long before the word became a part of the business lexicon.

INTRODUCTION

Neel was like the pole-vaulter who uses a flexible pole as a pivot to help scale heights he wouldn't have attained otherwise. The assurance of a soft landing helps the pole-vaulter take the risk. Neel's ability to pivot grew with time as the pole became more flexible and the landing pile thicker. The flexibility, representing greater fluidity of thought, allowed him to deviate even further from the beaten track. The rising landing pile increased his risk-taking ability.

Thanks to the habit of pivoting, in small and large measure, yet consistently, Neel landed in the right places and seized growth opportunities to get ahead of his peers, who often remained stuck in outdated models.

I am sure there is a Neel in you too, your Neel, and you can use Neel's story to peep into your own life.

To help you find him, I have shared questions at various junctures of the book. If you keep a pen/pencil handy while reading, you can discover your Neel by responding to these questions.

The questions also help break the book into bite-sized portions, consistent with the times when Instagram reels, TikTok and T20 are working in unison to reduce our attention span.

Books must adapt to the times, to not just survive, but with an aim to thrive.

Part 1

WHAT DO YOU WANT TO BE?

Neel wasn't the name given to him by his parents. Like most parents, Neel's parents had chosen a two-word name that summed up their unfulfiled desires, hopes and expectations for their only child. The name Neel came along the way because his friends, not wanting to invest more than a syllable or two in someone who they thought of as a placeholder for most activities, found it easy and simple to pronounce. The school hockey coach often asked him to kneel every time he failed to connect the ball during practice, which provided the context.

Neel was neither physically unfit nor mentally inactive. He cycled 5 kilometres from home to school and back every day, swam often and played chess. Yet he wasn't a fan of team sports. A bit of a loner, he liked to read; while other kids played ball games, Neel sat by himself in class with his nose buried in a book. He wasn't great at synchronised activities like march-past either. So, it came as no surprise that on the annual sports day, his teachers placed him in the last row, well behind the rest, to discreetly conceal his reluctant feet and flailing arms, which never moved in sync with the beating of the drums and skirls of the bagpipes.

In conclusion, despite being the apple of his parents' eyes, humans wouldn't have missed a beat if Neel hadn't been born.

Would you describe yourself as studious or sporty, a competitor or a participant, or a bit of both when you were in early school? What were the things you liked doing? What were you good at, according to others?

_____

_____

_____

_____

_____

_____

When Neel was young, his father would often take him along for an after-dinner walk. This window was intentionally created to discuss inspirational subjects that he thought would influence the boy's youthful mind and encourage him to build an honest and meaningful life. That's what success meant to any father in the 1960s.

On one such walk, his father asked Neel what he wanted to be when he grew up. While Neel struggled to answer, his father didn't wait long after he had asked the question. He suggested that Neel should consider becoming a doctor. Doctors alleviated human suffering, saved lives and improved people's health. Medicine, according to Neel's father, was a noble profession as it required a higher level of compassion, empathy and ethics compared to other vocations.

By the end of that walk, Neel's impressionable mind was convinced that, on growing up, he wanted to become a doctor. The very next day, he announced the decision to his friends at school, and everyone felt that, given Neel's inclination towards studies, it was the right thing for him to do. Simultaneously, he was cautioned about the limited seats available in medical colleges. One required high scores in competitive exams to gain admission to a reputed institute.

His father was happy that his son had listened to his advice, and at every family gathering, he'd ask Neel, 'What will Neel become when he grows up?' When Neel said 'Doctor!', everyone present would clap for him. This made his father smile from ear to ear as he proudly patted Neel on his back.

Many such instances pushed Neel to drop whatever little sporting activity he'd indulged in and divert all his time and focus towards studies. Soon, he was topping almost all his examinations.

Was there a profession you wanted to follow growing up? What inspired you to think this way? How did this affect your daily life?

_____
_____
_____
_____
_____
_____
_____

Neel was an only child, and everything at home centred around him. Never in his life did he have to share either belongings or attention, and he had his way in most decisions that concerned him at home.

His mother was one of six siblings and had grown up fighting for her space and voice in her home. She recognised the signs of Neel's growing entitlement and self-centred behaviour and was determined not to let him become a social misfit—someone incapable of resolving conflicts outside the safety of his home.

WHAT DO YOU WANT TO BE?

Were you an only child or did you have siblings? Do you know someone who had more or fewer siblings than you did? Did this change the way you and the other person turned out eventually?

_____
_____
_____
_____
_____
_____
_____

One day, when Neel was barely eight, he came home very upset. A neighbour's kid had hit him, offended by something Neel had said. Neel wanted his mother to speak with the boy's mother and have him reprimanded.

His mother thought for a moment and said, 'Neel, you're a big boy now. If you can't beat someone you've irritated because he's stronger than you, find another way to deal with the situation. Learn to solve your problems yourself.' After that, she pretended to go back to what she had been doing before.

So far, Neel had been accustomed to his parents' unconditional support. His mother's sudden change of heart and her indifference left him surprised and slightly bewildered.

Think about some early childhood memories. Did your parents' intervention when you faced difficulties, or the lack of it, help you own and solve your problems, or did you depend on others to solve them for you?

_____
_____
_____
_____
_____
_____
_____

The lack of sibling interaction made Neel somewhat of a loner despite his mother's conscious and continued attempts to engage with him. When his aunts and cousins came to visit their home, Neel would hesitate to speak up. He felt like an outsider in his own home, intruding on their private space. Every sentence he uttered made him feel as if he were seeking undue attention. He feared rejection and felt that even if they were in a great mood, they'd ignore him and continue with their banter. On days like these, he'd silently wait for the meals to get over and for people to leave so that he could be by himself again.

On one occasion, when three cousins stayed over and all the children were made to sleep in the living room, Neel shut his eyes and feigned sleep while his cousins enjoyed themselves. As they chatted into the wee hours of the morning, Neel waited for them to start talking about him and call him names. To his dismay he did not hear his name being mentioned even once.

Also, on such occasions, cousins would play the game of Seven Tiles in the courtyard of their home. The person whose turn it was had to break the seven tiles, stacked one on top of the other, with a ball. Once broken, his task was to put the tiles back together while the others hit him with the ball. He scored a point if he was able accomplish the task without being hit. When his turn would come, Neel's attempt would be to pitch the ball in a way that it was caught by someone, thus disqualifying him, instead of breaking the pile of tiles. He did not want to go through the precarious task of putting the tiles back together again while dodging the ball.

Were you an outgoing and proactive person while growing up, and the first to suggest what to do? Or did you wait for others to decide, while you followed? What drove your passive or charge-taking behaviour?

_____
_____
_____
_____
_____
_____

Neel's father did not have a very high-paying job. Even then, he insisted that Neel go to the best school in town. It was his father's way of making sure that Neel got what he'd missed.

Neel had always wondered why his family never went on summer holidays like some of his classmates. His school bag, plain and a little worn at the edges, stood out among the brightly coloured ones in class. He never said anything about it, even though he was conscious of it.

Once Neel turned fifteen and entered senior school, his father sat him down and explained the family's financial condition. He told Neel about how much he earned, what their key household expenses were and how much they had in the bank and other investments. All that information

WHAT DO YOU WANT TO BE?

rattled Neel a bit. He was aware that they were not rich, but he wasn't aware of their near hand-to-mouth state of existence. From his mother's expression, Neel could make out that she wasn't very pleased about his father having such a frank conversation with him. At one point, she couldn't hold herself back anymore and said, 'Why are you burdening the boy with such information? This has nothing to do with him!'

'So?' his father said, sensing the tension in the room. 'He should know we are not rich, at least not as rich as most of his classmates. However, I don't want him to feel inferior to anyone. We pay the same fees to the school as his friends do, and don't owe anyone any money. We could've sent him to another school that isn't as expensive, and that would have helped us live better. But we chose not to. Like most middle-class parents, we may not leave him with a large estate or even a fat bank balance. But we'll make sure he has had the best education, so he can achieve everything we couldn't—and more—by himself. We want his life to begin from where ours left off, or maybe even go higher. As long as he keeps that goal in mind, we don't need to worry about anything else. That's all we should hope for, and I want him to know that.'

That conversation with his father eliminated whatever feelings of inadequacy Neel had, and he started inviting his classmates over to his home without guilt or shame, something he'd hesitate to do before that day.

At what age did you get to know your family's income, expenses and reserves? What was your reaction?

_____
_____
_____
_____
_____
_____

As a toddler, Neel was a fussy eater. Long before Neel could read, his mother would read him a story to divert his attention while she fed him. Completely engrossed in the tale, Neel's mouth would be wide open, and his mother could feed him whatever she wanted. As he grew older, the stories evolved from fables about birds and animals to tales of kings, queens, noblemen and the occasional villain.

Once Neel learnt to read, his mother subscribed to a couple of children's magazines. Neel started slowly, but at an age when most kids would bawl often, break toys and write on walls, he'd finish a fortnightly magazine in only five days. His mother added more subscriptions, and Neel's appetite for reading kept pace with the growing stack of available magazines.

WHAT DO YOU WANT TO BE?

Encouraged by his mother, Neel could memorise and narrate each story. Sometimes, she would ask him to tell the tale he'd just read, but give it a different ending. He would do this easily.

Magazines soon gave way to storybooks, which were followed by novels as he moved up the grades. Neel was always the first in his class to read any new title, and his friends would check with him before starting a book themselves.

By the time Neel reached senior school, he spent most of his time after school with a friend who lived nearby and was a keen debater. Neel accompanied him to a couple of debating competitions and was impressed by how effortlessly his friend would understand the problem statement, analyse the facts and articulate his opinion crisply in a few powerful words. What surprised Neel the most was the fact that he could do this with equal conviction for either side of the motion.

Given how much he read, Neel felt that he was well aware of the world around him and could do all of that—perhaps even better than his friend. He started practising on his own, selecting random topics from newspaper headlines. His friends were surprised when Neel entered his name for the school debate. They'd never heard him speak much.

When a friend asked Neel if he was sure he wanted to participate in a debate—especially since he had never even taken up the mic at the school assembly—Neel said, 'So?

There can always be a first time. And if it doesn't work, I won't enter again.'

This was the first time any of his friends had seen Neel take a stand.

Do you remember the first time you took a stand that was based on your understanding of the situation and was contradictory to your behaviour in the past, hence startling you as well as those around you? What was it about and how did it make you feel?

_____
_____
_____
_____
_____
_____
_____

Neel emerged as the runner-up in the debate. Before long, he was heading the school's debating team, and his school began sweeping awards at every competition they entered.

Around this time, Neel's aunt visited from overseas, and she carried a jigsaw puzzle for him. Neel opened the box and emptied all the pieces onto the dining table. In no time, he had assembled all the 500 pieces of the jigsaw to recreate a beautiful picture of a London bus. His aunt, who was fond of

WHAT DO YOU WANT TO BE?

Neel, was so amazed at the speed with which the young boy had methodically solved a complex maze that she decided to send him more such puzzles every time she or someone else was travelling to India. Soon, Neel was solving jigsaws with 10,000 pieces, and a part of the family dining table was always reserved for the puzzle Neel was working on.

The familiar 'What do you want to be when you grow up?' act was played in front of Neel's aunt, too, during one of her visits. But unlike others, her response was not very encouraging. She believed that Neel was too young to decide his career and needed more exposure to figure out what he liked doing and where his strengths lay. She summed up her perspective succinctly: 'Where I come from, children enter college for a course in economics and graduate as a flautist. Neel is still years away from college.' She suggested structured aptitude tests that could help Neel make the decision. But Neel's father, who was her elder brother, brushed her off, saying, 'You Westerners are too rich and too structured. All you do is waste precious thought, time and money to complicate simple decisions in life.'

Were there activities other than the subjects you studied at school that you accidentally started and became better at than most others? Did these experiences make you rethink your career choice?

_____
_____
_____
_____
_____
_____
_____

In high school, Neel had to decide on his subjects. There was a pattern to the choices students made. The highest scorers picked science. Within the stream, boys picked engineering drawing, while girls chose biology. Commerce came next in the pecking order. Finally, the not-so-serious students were advised to take up the humanities. Given his grades, the obvious and conventional choice for Neel was the sciences, which he opted for. Considering he wanted to become a doctor, he picked biology. He ended up being the only boy in a biology class full of girls.

By now, Neel had been branded as hard-working, methodical and articulate. He was the teacher's favourite, and every teacher wanted to help him score well in the school-leaving exams. After all, Neel's success reflected on their ability to coach the students. For the same reason, they offered to help him prepare for the medical college entrance exams.

Meanwhile, Neel's friends were busy gearing up for engineering college entrance exams, struggling to figure out which branch they wanted to specialise in. Here, too, the high-ranking ones aimed for electronics and mechanical engineering, while those with lower marks picked other streams.

Neel felt a sense of relief. Unlike engineering, in medicine, the choice of specialisation had to be made at the time of enrolment for his master's degree.

Did students decide their subjects based on their rank versus their aptitude and interest when you were in school? Did you follow the convention too or did you exercise independent judgement?

_____
_____
_____
_____
_____
_____
_____
_____

Neel's uncle, Jay, his father's younger brother, was a successful lawyer who'd left his practice and had become a freelance educator. He taught courses at three universities and was always on the move, teaching students at law schools across the world.

Neel's father did not think much of Jay, often calling him a wasted genius who could have made more money and fame than he did. Neel liked Uncle Jay's company and tried to spend time with him whenever he visited. The affection was mutual.

On one such visit, after the usual 'What do you want to be when you grow up?' routine was over, Jay took Neel aside and asked him, 'Neel, what is your *purpose* in life?'

In that moment, Neel couldn't quite understand what Jay was asking. He was puzzled, just as any high school kid would be.

Understanding his nephew's confusion, Jay refined his question: 'What do you enjoy doing, and are you getting better at it?'

Jay went on to explain further, sharing his own story. 'I loved the complexities of the legal profession. Moreover, being a logical thinker and a sharp problem solver, becoming a lawyer felt like my natural calling. In hindsight, I realise that these traits could apply to any profession, but back then, I guess I was trying to build a case for myself to study law. It seemed like a logical fit.

WHAT WILL YOU LEARN?

'I worked very hard and fulfiled my dream. I became a successful lawyer. Yet, while I was scoring goals and making my clients win, I felt I was living mechanically, just moving from one victory to another. There was a lack of fulfilment in my life, a hollowness, as if something was missing. That's when I took a step back and introspected. I discovered that I enjoyed talking to others about my wins more than winning. I wasn't being pompous about my achievements—I just liked inspiring others to think like me and was happy to see them succeed, too. So, I dumped my lawyer's career and moved on to teaching law. I became a teacher who decides what he wants to teach, and I only teach people who want to learn and not the ones who are simply chasing a lucrative degree. I do not necessarily teach at a college that pays me the most, either. I make my choices, and I love what I am doing.

'You are still too young to understand the profound difference between a goal and purpose. A goal is finite. It is a destination. Destinations come and go. In contrast, purpose is a journey that does not have an end. Being conscious of this difference—whether it is the beginning of your career or while you are shaping it through the stages of your life—will help you move towards fulfilment. For now, ask yourself: What do I like? What am I good at? Which parts of it could lead me to a profession that I can step into with confidence? The rest will follow.'

'But Uncle,' Neel asked, 'I've already promised Dad that I will be a doctor, and he's told the entire clan. My friends know this, and I haven't even appeared for the engineering entrance exams.'

'*So?*'

That was all Uncle Jay said.

While this left Neel more bewildered than he was before, the conversation had stirred something in his subconscious. Neel realised that, although the world saw him as merely studious, his prowess with puzzles and debates could reveal that he was a logical problem solver with an articulate and extroverted personality. These were qualities aligned more naturally with an engineer's profile than that of a doctor.

Neel had recently met some of his seniors who had taken up medicine, and that's when he had realised that a five-year medical degree had to be followed by internships and post-graduation degrees, all of which took at least ten-odd years. In comparison, an engineering degree took less time, and the chances of getting a job at the end of an undergraduate course were better.

Neel's father was already fifty-five and had only five years before retirement. His conversation with Jay, coupled with the knowledge that a medical education was a rather drawn-out journey, made Neel conclude that he needed to *pivot* his career's direction from medicine towards engineering.

The timing was wrong. All entrance exams for engineering colleges were over, and a change of heart at this stage meant that his options would be limited to a handful of engineering colleges, which weren't ranked highly and

WHAT WILL YOU LEARN?

used school-leaving marks instead of an entrance exam as the selection criterion. Yet Neel was convinced that it was better to make the move now than regret it for the rest of his life. His conviction led him to abandon the medical dream he'd cherished for nearly a decade and pivot to engineering, even if it meant joining a not-so-great college.

His father was upset, and for the same reason Neel had once told Jay when he had popped the same question. Neel started with a '*So?*' and the conversation went through the expected stages of annoyance, anger, silence and pleading, till the family accepted Neel's logic, which he put forth with extreme patience, precision and rock-solid conviction. His debating skills came in handy.

Did you think of changing direction in your career in your early years? Could you make the change you wanted to?

_____
_____
_____
_____
_____
_____
_____

Did the clarity of your thought process, its articulation or the patience with which you handled the other stakeholders help? Or did you inform others, and they had no choice but to accept?

_____
_____
_____
_____
_____
_____
_____
_____

Part 2

WHAT WILL YOU LEARN?

Neel joined an engineering college in another town, and that took him away from home for the first time. It was not very far, yet far enough for Neel to visit home not more than once in three months, most times just for a long weekend.

College turned out to be different in more ways than one.

In school, Neel's academics and his debating skills had made him the teacher's pet. Here, everyone had been a topper in their schools. Moreover, state and national sports champions were studying alongside him. One of his batchmates was a stage performer who had played a small yet memorable part in a hit film. Then there were singers, guitarists, painters and drummers, too.

Soon, Neel understood that the size of the pond had remained the same. But here, he wasn't the only big fish, and getting noticed by his teachers or classmates wasn't going to be a cakewalk anymore. He had also lost all his accumulated credibility and had no choice but to start afresh. First, he needed to figure out who was worth impressing, and then come up with a plan to attract the attention of the ones he wanted to impress.

Did you ever have to struggle to attract other people's attention, at home or work? What feelings did the lack of attention leave you with? Did you simply live with the situation, or did you take action to get noticed?

_____
_____
_____
_____
_____
_____
_____

When Neel was at school, everyone was from the same city and had a similar social background. At college, students came from both cities and villages. Some spoke fluent English, while others struggled with it. He had peers who'd grown up in one city all their lives and those who'd moved three, four, even eight schools because their parents had transferable jobs. There were students from affluent homes and those who wouldn't have been here without a scholarship.

Neel's first instinct was to find people like himself—students who came from salaried middle-class homes in large cities and spoke English. Only five others fitted this description, and they seemed just as lost. It was only natural for them to flock together and hang out during lectures, mealtimes in the dining hall and even during their leisure hours. Soon, their group was branded as 'Yankees'. Even at the freshers' welcome party, the 'Yankees' became the subject of almost every skit or song that was performed.

At that event, one of the seniors, also from a similar background, took the Yankees aside and brought to their notice their isolation and the fact that they were being marked out by others. Neel's first response was 'So?'

The senior, though taken aback by a junior questioning him, took a deep breath and explained the situation. 'The purpose of college is not just higher education—you can get that through a correspondence course as well. This is an opportunity to live with and understand people from diverse backgrounds, absorb different perspectives and synthesise your worldview with what you see, hear and feel. It will help you get used to accepting things that you sometimes have no choice but to follow, willingly or unwillingly. And trust me, there will be many occasions in your life when you'll have to do that.

'Don't act like snails or frogs. Come out of your shells and wells and face the world in its rawest form, while you still don't have much to lose—because right now, you don't. If you miss this opportunity to learn how to behave in large groups, you will walk into a career unprepared and unarmed. In the big, bad world—that it certainly is—you risk being misfits for the rest of your lives.'

That strong message hit home, and the 'Yankees' were rarely seen together after that day, at least not in public.

Neel started sitting for meals with people he had once scoffed at. He soon realised that behind their unpolished communication lay minds that were way sharper than his own. It was not just about solving mathematical equations. Their views on social issues, economics, politics and policy, though diametrically opposite to what he'd subscribed to so far, made complete sense when seen through the lens of the milieu they had grown up in. By now, Neel had come to accept that he represented a minority, while most others belonged to the majority. It made sense for him not only to appreciate but also absorb their views. Soon, the conversations started to move from the dining hall to one of the rooms and would continue late into the night. The more Neel engaged with his new friends, the deeper his intrigue grew about the parts of the country he was hitherto unfamiliar with. Instead of visiting his parents over the upcoming long weekend, Neel decided to travel to his friend's village and continue with the immersion he'd only begun.

When his parents expressed their unhappiness, Neel said, 'So? I was home last month for six days, and I'll be back again in eight weeks for another week. Let me spend some time seeing how people who are not like us live.'

WHAT WILL YOU LEARN?

Was your core group at college made up of 'people like you' or was it a diverse group? Did your friends challenge your thoughts? In hindsight, would you have made friends with a different lot?

_____
_____
_____
_____
_____
_____
_____

The intense scrutiny that Neel experienced at school and home was lifted the day he entered college. Suddenly, there was no pressure to sleep and wake up at a designated time; no fixed uniform and haircuts; no one could force him to attend classes or stop him from going out. He could do whatever pleased him, and when he wanted to.

One evening, Neel went out for a movie with his friends, and they later stepped out for a meal. His friends ordered beers for everyone and lit cigarettes. Neel had never tried either. However, he was ashamed to admit it. When he debated whether he should drink and smoke, his mind simply said, 'So? You are old enough to try, and if you don't like it, don't do it again.'

He took small sips of his beer, figuring out with each sip if it did something to his head. He did not want to end up behaving like characters he had seen in the movies, walking out of bars in a drunken stupor. The beer did nothing except make his head feel a bit light. He continued. The first puff of the cigarette hit his throat so hard that he nearly choked. He covered it up by pretending that it was the beer that had accidentally gone down his windpipe. But his inability to inhale the smoke properly and the way he exhaled through the mouth gave away his inexperience. His friends spent the next couple of days teaching him how to smoke. Soon, Neel was going out for drinks with his friends on weekends, and he smoked often in the hostel.

Neel's new habits did not come cheap and were certainly unaffordable with the money his father sent him every month. Moreover, unlike most of his friends, who lit a cigarette only when they sat down with a beer maybe once a week or less, Neel found it difficult to switch on and off at will. He had become an active smoker and needed a packet a day to satisfy his urge. Even though he liked the feel of it, the price of sustaining this joy worried him no end.

Neel, aware of the hardships his parents were going through to take him through college, did not want to enjoy his new habits while they were cutting corners. He decided to take up tuition for school-going children in residential areas near his college. He'd teach thrice a week after classes, and that helped him fund his weekly outings and cigarettes. His conscience felt cleaner.

Did you pick up any unwanted habits as a youngster, in the absence of supervision and/or societal pressure? Did you regret them? If yes, were you able to shed them?

_____
_____
_____
_____
_____
_____
_____

At the end of the first year, three of Neel's classmates decided to leave the college. They were moving to another institute where they'd been admitted to the civil engineering stream. Since most civil infrastructure projects were carried out by the public sector, they felt this shift offered a greater possibility of landing a government job, which came with benefits like a post-retirement pension. The boys were willing to let go of a year of their lives and start afresh.

Neel gave it a thought and discussed it with his friends and his father. He gathered that while the government jobs accorded security and certainty, they lacked the flexibility which the private sector had to offer, both with respect to making decisions and personal growth. Not only was the private sector more efficient, but it also rewarded entrepreneurial behaviour, and those willing to stick their neck out made disproportionately high gains. Speaking to his friend, Neel summarised what he had understood so far, 'To me, a government job sounds like locking my money in a fixed deposit account with my bank, while the private sector seems like the equivalent of investing it in the stock market. Both are good, and the choice is determined by your appetite for risk-taking and the faith you have in your ability.'

He gathered that if anyone wanted to join the government, they should take a stab at the civil services examinations after completing their undergraduate studies. While the cadres were not devoid of bureaucratic mazes, they did promise more oversight and a broad span of control—far more than what a civil engineer posted to build a bridge or a dam in a remote location would ever achieve.

Neel set aside the thought for the time being and decided to revisit the subject once again after he had graduated and only if the lure of a secure government job ever came back to him.

WHAT WILL YOU LEARN?

Did you ever weigh the alternatives of the government and private sectors for a career? Which did you choose and why? Do you regret your choice?

_____
_____
_____
_____
_____
_____
_____

One day, the students at the engineering college heard of one of their favourite professors being hospitalised due to a sudden illness. The same evening, the news of his death arrived. Since the professor lived on campus, students went over to his house to pay their respects. This was the first time that Neel had seen a dead body and attended a funeral. The images stayed in his head for a long time, especially the empty coffin on the doorstep of the home, waiting for the teacher's body to be placed in it.

Around that time, Neel's father fell ill. His mother had to take him to the hospital twice a week for consultations and treatment. Neel spoke with his parents once a week and started visiting his home every month for a weekend instead of once in three months as he would do earlier. Each time, as he walked towards his home in the early hours of the morning after an all-night bus ride from college, he couldn't help but imagine a hearse parked at the door. As he got closer to his home, its absence came as a huge relief.

With every subsequent trip home, Neel saw his father become visibly frailer. Aware of the family's finances and reserves, the fate of his college education and his future had Neel endlessly worried. One night, when Neel was at home and couldn't sleep because of his father's laboured breathing, his mind started to spiral. He imagined the consequences of something happening to his father. He realised there was no way his remaining two years of college could be sustained in the absence of his father's salary.

That's when he said to himself, 'So? Will I give up on what my father has always worked towards and has wanted so badly?'

Neel decided to quit smoking and cut down on other expenses while continuing with the tuitions. He started washing and ironing his clothes himself, used the bicycle instead of the bus as often as he could and reduced the frequency of his outings. That helped him cut his monthly cash requirement by 20 per cent, and he asked his mother to send him that much less money every month. The reason he gave his mother for needing less money was that he had already bought his books at the beginning of the semester, and there weren't any more that were left for him to buy. In his mind, he was preparing for the worst—ready to apply for an education loan and complete his course if something were to happen to his father.

Did you face a major family crisis while growing up? How did you respond to it? Did it strengthen you, or did you become weaker as a result? Did the crisis change the course of your life for the worse, or did it help you step up to the challenge?

_____
_____
_____
_____
_____
_____
_____

It was mandatory for students to go for an eight-week training in a factory during the summer break between the third and fourth year. One evening, while chatting, Neel and another friend decided to take up additional summer training after their second year as well. They'd learn something new, make some money too, as this programme carried a small stipend, and wouldn't while away their vacations at home. Their placement coordinator, examining their unprecedented request, was pleasantly taken aback. He said, 'You guys surprise me, because most students consider the factory training as unnecessary and treat it like an unavoidable chore. We even receive many complaints of irregular attendance of summer trainees from the factories.'

'So?' Neel said. 'Just because some students have not seen value in the exposure doesn't mean that it is not useful.'

The coordinator did not have an answer to that.

The college had two vacancies remaining after placing everyone from the senior batch. Neel and his friend convinced the coordinator to allocate these positions to them, and he agreed on the condition that they sign an undertaking stating that this training would not be considered as a substitute for the mandatory formal training required after the third year. The boys were happy to do so, and off they went to a small town to spend the next two months working in a factory.

Living in factory accommodation for shift workers, eating frugal meals in the canteen and performing manual tasks for ten hours a day that included loading, unloading and monitoring the process parameters was certainly not the lifestyle the boys were accustomed to; it left them drained at the end of the day. Yet they felt very excited because it made them feel like responsible, grown-up adults who were going to work. Through the week, they'd work and look forward to their time off when they'd take a bus to a nearby town, grab a couple of beers, eat a hearty lunch at the local diner and watch the latest movie from the front row of a run-down non-air-conditioned theatre. The assignment gave them profound insights into how things worked in a factory, the life of factory workers, their limitations, aspirations and what kept them going.

Another benefit of the training, perhaps unknown and unintended, struck Neel only after he had returned to the college and resumed their classes. While other students would struggle to visualise the operations and processes of a manufacturing plant when these were being taught in class, Neel, having seen all of it first-hand, was already a step ahead. He was thinking about modifications and improvements that could be implemented and how this process would connect with other processes within a factory's ecosystem. The teacher would often be taken aback when Neel asked questions of this nature. Sensing that his knowledge base was now a step ahead of their classmates, the teacher often asked Neel and his friend to talk to the class about the practical aspects of what they were being taught, based on their work experience in the factory.

This enthused Neel, and he suggested to his teachers that they leverage their connections with the college alumni to arrange short, voluntary projects at factories in the vicinity. The teachers were happy to help, and this initiative turned out to be a big hit among all students. In addition to being a source of knowledge, they provided the batch an opportunity to step out of the campus and meet professionals.

By the time he reached his final year, Neel was back to being the teacher's pet, even though it was a small pond that was full of big fish. It's just that he was a bigger fish than those big fish.

Did you experiment with any offbeat activities in your youth that benefitted your learning and got you noticed as well? In hindsight, could you have tried some more?

_____
_____
_____
_____
_____
_____
_____

By now, Neel's father had recovered and was relatively better. He would write Neel a letter every alternate day, to which Neel responded at least once a week.

During Neel's final year at college, his father's letters focused on a single, recurring theme. At an office dinner attended by some of his senior colleagues, his father mentioned that Neel was in the final year of his engineering course. Many of them, having older children, shared their experiences. They believed that an engineering degree alone would confine Neel's domain to manufacturing, potentially stunting his career growth. In contrast, topping up the engineering degree with an MBA would elevate his prospects and open doors to roles in general management. This exposure could put him on a professional track with oversight not merely over manufacturing but many functions of an organisation. Hence, investing another two years now would yield significant returns over his thirty-five- or forty-year career.

After that evening, Neel's father's letters invariably would start by urging him to think about pursuing an MBA after his graduation. And he wouldn't stop there. He would push him to explore the best institutes, their admission dates and processes and the preparations he would need to undertake for clearing the entrance exam.

During his next trip home, Neel tried to reason with his parents. Citing the family's financial condition and the fact that his father would retire before the completion of Neel's post-graduation, he felt the need to take up a job as soon as he could instead of pursuing another academic degree. However, his father would hear none of this.

Neel smiled when his father started his response with a 'So?'—that one word made him feel that he'd lost the battle already. 'Another two years of funding your education is not such a big deal, considering the trajectory it would take your career into,' his father reassured him. 'I am an accountant, and I'd classify your education as an investment whose benefits will flow over the long term. I don't treat it as just an expense—which is what you are doing.'

Neel agreed to consider, but insisted on taking an education loan from a bank to fund part of the expenses rather than letting his father bear the entire burden. Initially, his father wouldn't hear of it, but he gave in after Neel cited the possibility of a higher starting salary after an MBA, allowing him to pay off the loan within a year or so of completing the course.

Uncle Jay was visiting home that week, and Neel got to discuss the subject with him as well. Neel's point was that all his efforts on a four-year engineering degree course would go to waste if he were to get into a management profession. He may as well have pursued a three-year degree in any other subject instead, if an MBA was what he planned to follow it up with.

'So?' Jay reasoned. 'Do you think all you learnt in engineering college was how to design machines and run factory operations? No! You don't realise it now, but the grind of those four years has trained you to distil any problem methodically, identify its various moving parts and solve them one part at a time until the entire issue is resolved. Without this degree, you'd have started gnawing at whichever part of the problem that caught your eye first—maybe even tried solving multiple parts at once—and would have messed it up even more.'

Once back in college, Neel mentioned his father's insistence to some of his classmates and was surprised to learn that many others were also toying with the thought. Yet they had not explored it any further since there were only a few good colleges with a handful of seats, and the entrance process was very tough. It comprised a written exam, a group discussion and an interview, reducing the chances of admission to way below bleak.

'So?' asked Neel. 'Didn't some of our seniors make it despite studying exactly what we are? Let's talk to some of them and see how difficult it was before we abandon the thought because of the fear of getting rejected.'

After consulting some seniors, Neel and his friends realised that while engineering had sharpened their mathematical skills, giving them an edge over students from other streams, they were at a disadvantage when it came to vocabulary, an area where liberal arts students excelled. Vocabulary, as it turned out, made up a significant portion of the entrance test and the time pressure of an engineering course had taken its toll—Neel had had no choice but to abandon his reading habit, ingrained while at school. The seniors who had successfully cleared the exam recommended a book called *Word Power Made Easy* by Norman Lewis as the go-to book for boosting their vocabulary.

The book had 1,500 new words, along with their meanings and suggestions for their usage. Neel and four others formed a small group and decided to work on improving their language skills together. They picked five to six pages of the book and went through them on their own during the day. Every night after dinner, they assembled to test each other on the words that they had read.

In three months, they knew the meaning of every word in the book, including tough words like 'megalomaniac', 'perspicacious', 'pulchritudinous', etc. Words that none of them had even heard before became a part of their everyday conversation.

Eventually, all five friends, of whom three had studied in vernacular village schools, got admission in more than one premium institute for a two-year, full-time MBA course.

Have you ever tried using the collective power of your group for an activity that initially seemed impossible, yet you were able to use it to make progress? In hindsight, is there something you could've done yet didn't?

_____
_____
_____
_____
_____
_____
_____

The first day inside the MBA classroom felt like a repeat of what Neel had been through four years ago at the engineering college. The room was filled with students from the best colleges and diverse disciplines, and considering that less than a per cent of applicants had made it, the calibre was on another level. But this didn't scare Neel. Having already been through the grind of proving himself once, he was confident. Moreover, he liked how well he was able to underplay the little anxiety he felt beneath a calm exterior.

If the engineering college had been less rigid than school, then MBA could be called 'laissez-faire'. No teacher dictated notes or read from a book or a chapter. They walked in, sometimes with a coffee mug in hand, and would start a conversation from anywhere. Students were expected to raise their hands and join the discussion at any stage they wanted. This routine continued until the end of each class, which would be concluded abruptly as it was time to move on to another class and another subject, but with a similar structure.

Case studies followed an identical pattern. You participated if you'd read the case. If not, you either listened and made notes for you to ruminate over after class. No one coaxed you into contributing; participation was left entirely to your initiative and desire to participate. One professor even went so far as to announce that students who weren't interested could leave after attendance had been marked. Most others allowed you to carry your coffee mug, a croissant or even light a cigarette if you wished.

The focus was on developing a perspective of your own, a point of view that you could defend, and on a good day, even get others to align with. Neel's background in debating came in handy, but he often felt out of his depth while arguing with students who had worked for a couple of years between their undergraduate degree and MBA. In moments like these, he wished he had done the same and not jumped from one degree to another. In addition to providing a fresh perspective, the experience would have also made him some money, eliminating the need to take a loan from the bank, which he was saddled with now. Sometimes when he felt low, he'd say to himself, 'So? Now that I'm here, there is no question of going back to work only to return. It is what it is, and I am where I am. Hence, all I can do is make the most of what we have at hand. Let me figure out how I can make up for the lack of experience.'

This realisation prompted Neel to read more. Instead of relying on textbooks alone, he shifted his focus towards business journals in his college library. Neel would spend most of his time there and read every international journal end to end.

During this process, it struck Neel that the articles that interested him most were closely related to human behaviour. He was inherently biased towards case studies that spoke about employees responding to changes in organisational structure, policies and incentives; consumers liking or dis-

WHAT WILL YOU LEARN?

liking advertisements, flavours and label designs; or price points and pack sizes that consumers rejected or welcomed.

We are exposed to an overload of information these days. Are you able to separate the content that pushes you to think more from the noise that helps kill time? Do you choose to consume more of the meaningful content, or do feel that noise is also necessary sometimes to relax the mind?

_____
_____
_____
_____
_____
_____
_____

The articles he read pushed Neel to check how reality correlated with the theory. He would walk into stores of all kinds—general, provision, as well as hardware and electricals—and talk to shopkeepers about products they stocked, what sold and what didn't. He would sometimes request the owners to allow him to sit in a corner and watch customers as they went through their stocks and made purchase decisions.

What intrigued Neel most was how factors like the price a customer was willing to pay, the value they placed on the reputation of the brand, the reliance on the shopkeeper's suggestion and the time they would spend before buying a product varied significantly across product categories. To think that people spent more time or sought more opinions before buying a refrigerator than a shampoo would be putting it simplistically, because they didn't.

To grasp the reasoning behind these decisions, one had to dig deep into the minds of customers, where they carefully weighed various criteria, applying different weights depending on both the individual and the product in question. Neel was fascinated by how customers navigated these decision trees, moving up and down their branches with nuance and thought.

He believed that the varied responses among employees to the same policy and structural changes were equally layered and were driven by the complex human decision-making process. But unlike the shops he sat in often, he did not have access to a vantage point that would allow him to observe these behaviours from up close.

So, when the time came to pitch himself for the summer training stint, Neel spotted an opportunity. He chose a manufacturing firm instead of a consumer marketing firm. He felt that this would give him insight into organisational policies and their impact on people and their productivity, while working with a marketeer would immerse him in the marketplace, an area he was already familiar with in theory through informal exposure.

His placement cell questioned this call: 'We thought you were specialising in marketing. Aren't you wasting your chances of getting a pre-placement offer by training in a factory?'

'So?' Neel reasoned. 'Why should the reasons behind people embracing or rejecting certain organisational processes or policies be fundamentally different from the reasons for which they like or dislike a brand, or accept or reject a price or a proposition?'

The placement coordinator wasn't convinced, and his confused face revealed that he found Neel's logic quite convoluted. But he decided not to argue.

Neel did not regret his decision. While the two summer jobs during his engineering course had focused on the manufacturing processes, he ensured that this assignment allowed him to observe his surroundings with a wider lens, helping him capture insights into people's behaviour. What he saw left him even more intrigued about human behaviour than his visits to the marketplace had been.

Write down the price of a kilogram of tomatoes, a litre of cooking oil, a cylinder of LPG gas and the cheapest bus ticket for the local bus in your city. Now, check your answers online for accuracy.

Next, guess the monthly salary of your building's security guard or any other migrant worker in your vicinity. How much money does he or she send home every month, and how many people does that money support? Ask him or her the real numbers tomorrow.

How connected with reality were you? If more than three of your answers were wrong, you need to walk the aisles of neighbouring stores and talk to your support staff more often.

_____
_____
_____
_____
_____
_____
_____

While Neel took an interest in every subject that was taught during his MBA, he sailed through operations management because of his engineering background.

WHAT WILL YOU LEARN?

He studied economics because he had to and thought investment management lacked a soul. His favourite was organisation development and consumer behaviour, simply because they studied people and why they did what they did. Neel never missed a class and frequently spoke to the professors and teachers after the class was over.

In the final exams, Neel topped both subjects. He supported his answers with solid theoretical reasoning and richly illustrated them with copious real-life examples—these came from what he had read in the journals, observed during the long hours he sat in the shops and what he learnt during the summer job studying people processes.

Alas, the placement season was a big disappointment. This was the era when almost every service, be it airlines, insurance, banking, hospitals, you name it, was run by the government. All that remained in the private sector was soaps, paints and a few consumer products. Neel was looking for a role in a consumer marketing firm, and the specific firm that he had his sights set on decided to cancel its visit after sharing the names of its shortlisted candidates. Neel's name had appeared on that shortlist, and he had been hopeful of joining them.

The other consumer marketing firms that Neel appeared for did not ask any questions related to consumer behaviour. Instead, they probed to evaluate if the candidates were curious, if they could handle diversity, how they responded to ambiguity, disruption, etc. Neel was not prepared to handle questions of this nature and fumbled his way through these conversations. He did not make the cut.

Later that night, he reflected on what had been asked of him. The answers did come to him, but it was too late. He was also upset that the placement cell, as well as his seniors, had not shared any advice on the kind of questions that were expected in such interviews.

'So?' he asked himself. 'Should I let it go since my season is over, or should I do something so that the future batches don't walk into interviews blindfolded like I did?'

Neel reached out to the placement cell and suggested that their role wasn't just limited to getting the best potential employers to the college campus. They should also investigate the firms' expectations from the candidates, maybe by consulting alumni working there. Additionally, they should create a question bank by collecting interview questions from candidates over time. This data, if collected over the years, would help prepare the students for their placement interviews.

He went a step further and added that while the college provided a marksheet that assessed students based on their academic performance, students could also be evaluated on behavioural traits like willingness to collaborate, ability to handle ambiguity, build and sustain teams, appetite for risk, ability to rise after hitting a roadblock, etc. Having observed them closely for two years during classroom interactions and project groups, the professors were better equipped with data and insights to carry out the scoring process as compared to the interviewers, who met the candidates for about fifteen minutes.

Since he was not interested in banking or technology, Neel settled for a job in a large firm that manufactured paints and was a market leader in the category. Under the circumstances, this was the closest he could get to understanding more about consumer behaviour in his first few years of working.

Should colleges provide a report card for attitudinal traits, too? Would teachers have enough exposure to these traits to assign these scores? If you were rated on attitudinal traits like curiosity, ambiguity, disruption, etc., at the end of college, how would you have fared?

_____
_____
_____
_____
_____
_____
_____
_____

Part 3

WHAT WILL YOU DO?

Neel joined the company shortly after the course ended. He was going through the induction when the firm that had cancelled their visit to the campus contacted him and suggested they meet. Neel's first response was, 'I'm sorry, I've joined the other firm, which had made me an offer on campus, only eight days ago.'

'So?' the caller said. 'We got the impression from your application that we were your first option. Also, are you planning to retire with this firm?'

Neel met them that evening, and a short interview later, was handed a typewritten offer by the interviewer who did not want to leave anything to chance. Given the eagerness with which the firm that had been his first choice was wooing him, Neel accepted the offer.

Neel was overjoyed with the change, and he wrote his resignation after just eight days of joining his first job. He called his parents to share his excitement, but was surprised to hear a sense of worry in his father's voice once he broke the news. His father couldn't understand how Neel could decide to move on from his first job after a week, while he had spent forty years in one firm. He asked if Neel had upset his manager over something. Once Neel assured him that that wasn't the case, came the next question: 'Is the new job paying you more?'

Neel explained that while the new job would pay 15 per cent less than his earlier job did, he preferred it because while the previous company made paints for walls, his new employer made paints for the face, nails and lips among other products, which had more frequent usage and purchase occasion opportunities versus paint. His father only heard '15 per cent lower salary' and did not understand the rest of the message. By now, his father's doubt—that Neel had failed to live up to the expectations of his manager—had become a certainty. Although the call did not end on a very pleasant note, Neel was confident that with time, his father would understand why he had made the switch.

Do you agree with what Neel did? Would you have done the same, too? If not, why not?

_____
_____
_____
_____
_____
_____
_____

Neel had worked towards being employed for many years; so, securing a job in a firm of his choice did give him that real kick. Yet, there was a lifestyle change that he had to get accustomed to.

WHAT WILL YOU DO?

The first year of training was particularly tough, as Neel had to relocate four times across the country. In the process, he was made to report to four different managers: one he classified as nice, two were bad and one was very bad. This evaluation was based on how they delegated tasks: whether they took the time to explain, gave orders without offering any guidance or just barked commands. One even threw a file he had brought for the meeting towards the door and asked him to carry it with him on his way out.

Neel was no longer his own boss. He had to wake up when necessary, not when he chose to, travel long hours, meet people who were driven by motives different from his own and negotiate mutually beneficial deals with them. He had to keep his manager regularly updated so his manager could inform his manager too, deliver on objectives set by someone else and repeat this cycle. Neel had no time to meet his batchmates who were posted in the same city as he was, as they too were caught up in an equally gruelling routine.

On a few evenings, Neel bought a quarter bottle of cheap whisky and consumed it all by himself. In those moments of silence, he overheard a debate between his heart and his head. His heart would ask, 'Is this what my father wanted me to do while he toiled and saved to pay for an engineering and a management degree, while I burnt the midnight oil? All I'll do is work with no time to relax or spend with people of my choice.'

'So?' his head countered. 'What else did you think you'd do? Sit in an air-conditioned room and order coffee? The guys who are doing that right now are older and have seen many seasons. If you don't trust their judgement, and therefore, their decisions, or if you feel they are not behaving as they should, all you can do is to not behave like them when you get to their level. That way, your teams won't think of you like you're thinking about them now. However, to reach the position where you can exercise that option, you have no choice but to go through today.'

Neel would then pour himself another drink and say, 'Maybe I'll change my mind by the time I am their age, too.'

If you are working, was there ever a mismatch between what you thought life would be after studies versus what it turned out to be? In what ways was it better or worse? If you are a student, what are your expectations for life after you start working? Should Neel have quit or rebelled instead?

_____
_____
_____
_____
_____
_____

WHAT WILL YOU DO?

Neel's initial couple of years after training were spent in operations, mainly sales. While he was barely twenty-six, most of his direct reports were forty or older and had risen through the ranks. While Neel spent most of his day reviewing sales reports prepared by his team members, he also worked on plans that required long hours of totalling numbers in rows and columns on his Casio fx-31 calculator. If the row and column didn't match, he would start all over again until they did. Only after the sheets were manually filled with numbers and the totals tallied could he examine parts of the data and find patterns, which they would call *insights*. Action plans came at the final stage, and it was usually very late in the night when he had the time to think about the 'what next' part of the plan.

The sales team often complained about the targets set by the head office, calling them arbitrary and rigid. On one occasion, a team member complained, 'These marketing guys know nothing about the market, yet they set our targets. Has any one of them ever gone to a dealer and sold a thing? Do they even know what the market size for our products is?'

'So?' Neel replied. 'If they don't know, who should be explaining it to them? And before we do that, we must be sure that we know about it ourselves.'

They agreed to set up a team to assess the real market size. Its members would collate data during the week and meet every Friday to discuss their findings. On the first

Friday, they showed a 40 per cent share for themselves amongst four competitors. Neel asked if there was a dealer in every part of the territory, or was the industry missing out on a lucrative sales opportunity by being unavailable where the customer was. This was easy, and the next Friday, they came up with a map of the territory with dealers marked. They had also identified blank spaces without dealers and projected a potential upside of 5 per cent over what they were selling by creating dealers in these spaces.

Next, Neel challenged the team to identify people who needed to take care of their skin—a need their product could fulfil—but were meeting it instead through alternate products. The team struggled to grasp this insight; since they'd been in the industry for a long time, they were under the impression that they understood it well by now. Neel suggested they go meet customers and dealers, especially in areas outside their sales hotspots, and specifically ask them questions about their purchasing decisions. He even offered to join them on some of these visits.

Two weekly meetings later, it was clear that there wasn't just one but quite a few alternate ways people were taking care of their skin. These included locally manufactured brands of poorer quality being sold in small shops tucked away in lanes and by lanes. There, products were available at half their price or even less.

It would be impossible for them to even produce at the price that the smaller players sold. Their formulation used inferior-quality raw material, and they had no overhead whatsoever. Giving it a thought, Neel said, 'So? Should we decide what the customer must pay for their needs, or should we try and produce something at a price they can afford? Imagine if these smaller brands we are calling inferior were to improve their quality by even a notch and creep into our market—wouldn't they eat into our share and take away some of our customers? Why don't we do the reverse by introducing a cheaper product and expanding our distribution to the shops they sell out of?'

The team wasn't convinced by Neel's argument. After all, it was the marketing team that made product decisions, and sales only sold the products they got. Then, Neel explained, 'Marketing is like the air force, and sales are the company's foot soldiers. Sales will need to tell marketing about the situation on the ground for which they need air support. Those flying up there can't guess by themselves what the foot soldiers need. Someone needs to tell them, and that someone is us.'

The team agreed, albeit half-heartedly, to collect samples of these alternative products and estimate potential sales volumes if a new product were priced midway between their own and the cheaper brands. However, they were clear that the proposal would not even be considered by the marketing guys.

After submitting the proposal, Neel invited a few colleagues from the marketing team to visit. He took them through the markets, showing them the quantities that were stocked by small dealers to give them a sense of what could be selling. He capped the day by presenting a projection of sales in the event they had a near-matching proposition and left it to the marketing team whether to launch it under the existing brand or create a new brand. The visiting team was surprised to see a projected doubling of sales in the territory.

At the quarterly sales conference, Neel reiterated the projected numbers to the country sales head and handed him some samples of the cheaper product. He requested him to have a word with the country marketing head, who was his colleague at the head office.

The sales manager was initially sceptical; what if their low-priced product cannibalised their existing volumes instead of growing the market? Neel responded, 'So? Will we wait until the smaller companies start eating our lunch? If that happens, the only option we'll be left with will be to defend whatever's left. We have a strong brand, which is aspirational, and my gut says that if we were to offer a lower-priced product, we might lose a few of our customers who sit on the fringes, but our gains will outweigh those losses. We can always run a small test in an isolated territory before going all the way.'

That argument made the sales manager support Neel's perspective at the head office.

WHAT WILL YOU DO?

Do your peers or team members complain about the tasks or the targets assigned to them? Do you see an opportunity to convert these complaints into an opportunity to grow, instead of joining the chorus, just as Neel did?

_____
_____
_____
_____
_____
_____
_____

It took a year to launch the new product range, during the time they targeted the dealers and customers they had previously missed. Their competitors followed suit. The industry expanded as major players introduced and advertised an affordable product. The small brands continued as before, but since Neel's firm had led the initiative, they gained the most and their sales had doubled.

The outcome was strong, yet the process went through hiccups. Earlier, the more expensive product would sell in high volumes through a handful of large dealers who had the money to hold inventory. In contrast, the new, comparatively affordable range was sold through a larger number of small dealers, who had trouble buying stock because of money and space constraints. This meant more frequent service visits, resulting in higher costs for the distributors who asked for a higher servicing margin, which the company declined.

Reports started pouring in about arguments between the sales team and the distribution partners. Some partners resigned, and a few were terminated. One day, a dismissed partner walked into a dealership and assaulted a salesman during a sale. As he left, he told the salesman who was lying on the floor, writhing in pain, 'Go tell your boss that if he can kick us in the stomach, so can we. This is our market because we built it. Till you don't agree to our new terms, anyone coming here will meet the same fate.'

Word reached Neel, and his immediate reaction was to drive 50 miles to the market and assess the situation first-hand. The area manager felt that the partner was overreacting because he'd lost his business just a week ago. Drawing on years of experience, he was sure that the man was likely to retaliate and could hurt anyone who entered the area so soon after this incident. He advised Neel, 'Let us lie low for a few days. The situation will defuse by itself, like it has in the past after similar incidents. This is not the first time that a partner who's been sacked has reacted badly.'

'So?' Neel said. 'Just because we have behaved like cowards in the past doesn't mean we should continue to do so. In a moment like this, it is our priority to make our team believe that they are not alone. We need to let the dealers know that they are dealing with us via our partners and aren't at our partners' mercy. Not responding immediately will create a permanent trust deficit within our teams and with the trade.'

Reluctantly accompanied by the area manager, Neel visited the spot that very afternoon, met with a few dealers in the vicinity and told everyone that henceforth, anyone taking the law in their own hands would be formally reported to the police. This had never happened before, and the incident was discussed at gatherings of sales teams and dealers and even across industries for days to come.

Have you or those you know faced a strong backlash to a change you proposed or made that forced you to rethink the change or even take it back? What did you do?

_____
_____
_____
_____
_____
_____
_____

Do you think it was wise on Neel's part to visit the market soon after his salesperson was assaulted? What would you have done?

_____
_____
_____
_____
_____
_____
_____

The violent incident at the dealership convinced Neel that there was something fundamentally amiss with the margin structure of the dealers, else they wouldn't have resorted to violence. He felt that it needed discovery and resolution. To probe further, he spoke to their loyal distribution partners as well as some young and articulate team members. He learnt that the distributors had added more manpower to service the new dealers, and they believed that the incremental margin earned from these sales was lower than the extra cost of servicing them. This was making them unhappy.

Neel ran the numbers for a couple of partners. Interestingly, he did not see a huge upside for the partner, but didn't spot a loss either. The distributors' negative attitude was based on a misconception. He concluded that it was

WHAT WILL YOU DO?

his team's inability to objectively convince the partners that was to blame. He approached the training manager, who agreed to work on the sales team's communication skills.

Training sessions started in the following week in small batches. Neel sat through one of them only to realise that the participants were simply being taught general probing and objection-handling skills. This wasn't the time for niceties. They were in the middle of a crisis, and the situation needed a cure, not a palliative. When asked, the training manager explained that the role of training has always been focused on boosting the team's basic management and communication skills, while specific issues were addressed in the field by line managers.

'So?' Neel questioned. 'Just because you've worked in silos during peacetime doesn't mean you can continue doing so when a crisis looms large. We need to evolve with the times. Since the line managers are aware of the problem and you are communication specialists, why can't you work together to produce the course material? You could even coach a couple of articulate line managers to deliver the message to frontliners, with you present.'

The training team was overwhelmed by Neel's unusual ask and reluctantly took up the challenge. Neel sat through the first meeting to kick-start the process, after which he left them to work independently. Within a week, the teams had a solution. The line managers designed a format to record the partners' return on investment, which the sales frontliners were to fill monthly in the presence of the partner and with the data that he provided. It covered investment in stock, infrastructure, market credit; expenses like rent and salaries; and return, which was essentially margin on sales. The training team created a document outlining the soft skills salespeople needed to remember while asking for this data and challenging false figures. This was followed by a plan to coach them on conducting objective conversations to help partners see that they were making a fair return on their investment with the support of a jointly prepared sheet.

The area managers thoroughly enjoyed teaching these concepts to their teams. They felt confident and respected and even believed the new-found knowledge boosted their resumes since it was applicable to several industries. After the role-play exercises, frontliners felt better equipped to manage the partners, and the training team was happy that they contributed differently and more effectively.

WHAT WILL YOU DO?

Do you have a conflict between two functions or between your company and its partners that could be resolved by the two arms working together to deliver a solution, just like Neel made Training and Sales collaborate? How would you go about it?

_____
_____
_____
_____
_____
_____
_____

Word about Neel's insightful and disruptive suggestions spread throughout the entire firm. At the annual sales conference, Neel was cornered by the company's CEO and offered a move to the marketing function. He was told that the offer was being made because Neel had gone above and beyond his immediate role and displayed strategic skills, which, if nurtured, could accelerate his career.

Thanking him for the opportunity, Neel politely declined. He said, 'I need to work in the trenches for a few more years before playing the strategy game, which I believe marketing is all about. Meanwhile, I understand that the firm wants to expand to select neighbouring countries by introducing more relevant products and setting up an infrastructure for their distribution. If I could be considered for a position in that team, it would expose me to new cultures and the rigours of fine-tuning our current products to suit the needs of customers in these regions, while building new teams and continuing to run operations.'

The CEO promised to consider Neel's request, then asked about his long-term plans. Neel replied that he planned to work for a few more years—maybe ten—to learn more about organisations and their processes, after which he planned to start something of his own, though he wasn't yet sure what that would be.

The CEO said, 'Neel, if you want to become an entrepreneur, I'd suggest that you resign tomorrow morning and take the plunge. It's better that you learn from your failures than from procedures that are followed by large firms. Also, the longer you stay, the more you'll get caught in a perk trap. Eventually, the cushy benefits will make it impossible for you to travel by train instead of flying, stay in budget hotels and or live without company-paid comforts. Moreover, you will not learn to manage the various ancillary processes that are carried out here by the support staff, which we take for granted, while entrepreneurs manage every function of organisations like ours single-handedly. Once you get used to this life and you have a family, your habits and responsibilities will make it impossible for you to take the plunge. Think about what I've said and take a call before it is too late.'

WHAT WILL YOU DO?

That night, Neel mulled over his CEO's words. In the end, he decided to wait for a response to his request for a shift to the international business unit before taking the call.

Do you think anyone wishing to become an entrepreneur should take the plunge before accumulating sufficient work experience?

_____
_____
_____
_____
_____
_____
_____
_____

The entrepreneurial call was put on the back-burner because the very next week, Neel was moved to the international business team and began reporting to the head of the business and one of the oldest hands at the firm. Somewhat old-school, this man made no bones about the fact that he was the boss, expected unconditional loyalty, insisted that no activity or initiative be executed without his knowledge or permission and that nothing should be shared outside the unit. The firm's decision to appoint someone of his age and management style to head a new business unit—where the task was to innovate and not just operate—surprised Neel.

However, he decided to go along with the flow and create room for himself by earning his manager's confidence.

It took Neel a couple of months to convince his manager that he was a loyal confidant. All Neel had to do was talk less and listen more, which signalled respect for his manager's knowledge and experience and a willingness to learn from him.

Once the trust had been established, his manager did not come in the way of Neel as he travelled to the markets, shortlisted two small countries for the initial test launch and shared insights from the visits with the marketing team that helped them create new products. He collaborated with R&D to create fresh formulations, worked with the purchase department to find new vendors for raw and packaging materials and finally with factories to gain priority for manufacturing and shipping. Meanwhile, Neel also appointed distribution partners in the two countries, and they were ready to launch.

While doing all this, Neel would keep his boss apprised every step of the way. He did this not just as a heads-up, but also to seek his advice. Neel's preparation was so thorough that after a while, there were very few inputs the boss had to offer, and he encountered negligible interference in his day-to-day activities, too.

Neel simply had to ensure that he created a weekly progress report covering every front, which his manager would send to the firm's CEO under his signature. Neel would also

WHAT WILL YOU DO?

place his manager on the dais at any launch and make him the spokesperson for every media interaction. To Neel, this was a small price to pay for the kind of independence and the exposure he was getting—something a twenty-eight-year-old could only dream of.

The two years that Neel spent on this assignment may have been tiring, yet the learning he accumulated was equivalent to six years elsewhere. The experience was not limited to just one dimension, such as sales or marketing. It gave Neel an overview of every function in an organisation and the interplay between them that was required to create and sustain a business. Interacting with international suppliers from countries where technology and communications infrastructure were at least five years ahead also opened many new possibilities in Neel's mind.

Do you approve of Neel's approach to gain his boss's confidence? Would you have complained about your boss's behaviour or considered quitting to find another job?

_____
_____
_____
_____
_____
_____
_____

Neel was aware that going forward, international business would eventually become business as usual with limited room for incremental learning opportunities. He considered asking for a transfer back to the domestic business, but the near-premium nature of the category left little scope for expanding distribution reach and consumption beyond what Neel had already attempted and succeeded in doing.

Neel was now on the lookout for another product category with broader acceptance—one that allowed greater potential for experimentation and growth. He began taking calls from headhunters, and within a month, an opportunity came his way which seemed worth exploring.

Neel joined a business that dealt in physical goods too, yet its products were priced lower and had a broader appeal. The firm had been growing by converting a commodity product to a brand, its core premise being consistency of quality. While wanting to create the brand, the family-run business had, for a couple of decades, stayed focused on matching the price of their packaged product with the commodity market price. This approach ran counter to the very idea of branding, and it was no surprise that they managed to convert less than 10 per cent of the commodity customers into purchasing packaged, branded products.

The next generation of the family that took over the business was smarter and quickly concluded that to change the landscape, the first need was to change the thinking, followed by the processes. This realisation led them to hire

WHAT WILL YOU DO?

Neel and many others with hands-on experience in the branded consumer goods sector. Neel was to head sales for a territory that contributed to almost a quarter of their business.

After joining, Neel consulted a few friends who were familiar with the firm and the industry, and he was advised to let go of his entire team if he wanted to make any headway. 'If you don't do that, you'll be setting yourself up for failure,' they said. So, in he walked like a surgeon, ready to remove the damaged organ responsible for the rot and to give a new lease of life to the dying patient.

The home-grown team were hesitant communicators, and they primarily used data to create reports that were filed and never leveraged to make any decisions. They were visibly in awe of the new entrant who had come from a much more pedigreed background. The organisation's rigid command-and-control environment, where no one challenged those above them, gave Neel a sense that he had joined the army. Just as Neel had walked in, sharpening his knives with a clear mind to slay the turkeys, the team, too, viewed his joining date as Thanksgiving.

After a couple of meetings—more informal than formal—the frost began to thaw, and the warm human beings behind the ice-cold exteriors slowly surfaced. Emotions occasionally showed; at first, only joy, as expressing dismay or disapproval required a huge sense of security, which takes a lot longer to build.

Neel observed in the team a desperate need to prove their prowess in the marketplace and an extreme hunger for knowledge. They'd remember every new theoretical concept that Neel wrote and illustrated on the whiteboard, ask questions to delve deeper and proudly demonstrate its application during his subsequent field visits. They were visibly hungry for Neel's appreciation, and their eagerness to earn his approval was all that seemed to matter to them in the moment.

When he realised that his team members were much more forthcoming in informal interactions, Neel stopped sitting at the head of the table during meetings and would just perch himself on a side cabinet or take a chair amidst them. This helped lower their guard and allowed their thoughts to emerge and move with greater fluidity.

On one such occasion, when a renowned consumer marketing firm with strong distribution muscle tried to enter their category, panic spread through the company—they were the only brand at risk of losing market share. As the launch date came closer, a few people from Neel's team resigned, only to appear across the border the very next day. Neel was worried too, but he maintained his cool since he didn't want the fear to percolate down through his team. He took his direct reports out for a drink to ease the tension and, more importantly, to get their thoughts on possible and quick defence strategies that could be deployed sooner rather than later.

WHAT WILL YOU DO?

Over drinks, ideas that ranged from unimplementable to ineffective started flowing. While everyone laughed, Neel remained serious yet humoured every suggestion to keep the conversation going. Finally, someone asked, 'How long does a company of their size plan to run an advertisement campaign for a launch of this magnitude?'

'Two months. Maybe three, if they get a good response,' Neel answered.

'That means we would be at our most vulnerable for roughly three months. We can't stop them from launching their product or spending a lot on advertising, but we can render that spend ineffective by blocking the dealer warehouses and shelves. One way of doing that is somehow persuading every dealer to stock three months' worth of our product just before their launch. That way, when they come selling, the dealers might only buy a token amount from them—certainly not enough to create a visual impact on the customers when they walk into the store. That should help us tide over the period when their advertising would be in full flow.'

Neel held on to the thought and urged the team to build on it. By the end of the evening, they had a plan to block the shelf space by selling three months' worth of offtake to every dealer. It would cost them 10 per cent of what they'd sell in discounts and spend on hiring dealer shelves. Nonetheless, the potential permanent loss of market share and the opportunity to advance sales more than justified the extra cost. The team too seemed raring to go out and implement the plan since they had conceived it.

The next morning, Neel sent a fax to his manager in the head office detailing the plan and received his approval over the phone within an hour. He assured him of extra stocks to fill dealer shelves while replicating the plan in all other regions, too.

Not only did the activity save them from a loss of share and face, but the quarter also saw an unprecedented growth of the branded industry versus commodity, across the country.

Have you faced a moment that threatened your existence? Did you plan a response or did you focus on just cutting your losses?

_____
_____
_____
_____
_____
_____
_____
_____

Neel was felicitated at the next annual day and was privately asked to move to the largest region in the country, an offer that initially scared him. The geography wasn't just the company's and the brand's home ground, but his

WHAT WILL YOU DO?

new office would be collocated with the head office. The thought of sharing the same space with seasoned senior managers of the firm did intimidate him. He also feared that the opportunity to boost sales in that area would be smaller because the brand had been there for far longer than in other regions. Hence, it was likely that most of the commodity-to-branded conversion had already happened.

The reality that Neel faced was the absolute opposite of his expectations. His first week in the new region felt much like the initial days in his earlier role—in terms of people, their confidence, processes and the state of the market. Neel chose to replicate his earlier approach step by step, avoiding what had not worked earlier and adding what he thought could have been done before, yet wasn't. The outcome was better because the size of the commodity industry in this region was much larger, and it was ripe for conversion to packaged and branded consumption.

It was during this time that desktop computers were introduced. Lotus 1-2-3 helped Neel create spreadsheets, while Freelance made presentations easier and more impactful. These tools saved him long hours of manual work, replacing the calculator for planning and acetates for presenting. The computer could be connected to an overhead projector, allowing cinema slide-like outputs to be shown to an audience. As a result, Neel had more time to spend in the markets, understand customers, dealers and processes and create more effective plans after in-depth discussions with the team.

The next sixteen months passed like a breeze, and his collocation with the head office provided him access, during the day as well as after hours, to senior management across functions. These interactions helped him learn more about strategic issues and interdepartmental coordination. This, too, was diametrically opposite to what he had feared. He gained access to the CEO, and while they didn't get to converse much, the proximity created enough interaction opportunities.

Have you faced a situation where the reality turned out to be the opposite of the expectations you had, pleasantly or unpleasantly? How did you respond?

_____
_____
_____
_____
_____
_____
_____

The training manager quit the firm, and when Neel walked up to the CEO and asked for the role, he was taken aback by Neel's proposition. The incumbent was much junior to

WHAT WILL YOU DO?

Neel, and moving into this role would be a regressive and career-limiting move.

'So?' Neel said convincingly. 'Maybe he was right for the role while we were skimming the surface. However, my experience of managing two of our four regions tells me that we have many best practices operating in various parts of the country that need to be discovered and codified into standard processes. To seize the next level of market opportunities, we will need to train people not just in selling skills but in fostering an attitude that motivates our teams to explore more opportunities. I can assure you that based on what we do in the time I am in the role, someone of my experience, or even higher, will ask for this job when I am ready to move on.

'Moreover, the move to a support function after eight years of handling line jobs will give me an opportunity to consolidate my learnings too,' continued Neel.

Neel's remarkable clarity of thought and confidence left the CEO and the HR head with no choice but to grant him what he wanted. Neel's colleagues, however, were slightly baffled. They felt that training was an area where non-performers were sent kicking and screaming, or for those who were averse to chasing targets. This wasn't the place for a person with Neel's track record, who deserved the country sales head role in a year, if not a few months. Meanwhile, Neel was already thinking about his next moves so that he could hit the ground running.

Would you make an unconventional career move like Neel did? If not, why?

_____
_____
_____
_____
_____
_____
_____

Neel had read and was impressed by Marshall McLuhan's *Understanding Media*, a book introduced to him by his professor in college. The book emphasised that the way we access information shapes our perception of it, sometimes even more than the information itself. Currently, monthly newsletters, printed on glossy paper, were being sent out to the sales folk across the country. Instead of continuing with this, Neel began to think of a new, more exciting medium of instruction.

He noticed that relatively compact handheld cameras with small cassettes had started replacing the bulky video cameras. Neel invested in one and started carrying it with him during his market visits across the country. He also connected with a local film editor who shot, edited and delivered recordings of weddings and other such social events on VHS cassettes.

WHAT WILL YOU DO?

During the six days each month that Neel spent in markets and in meetings with dealers and salespeople, he would capture on film any interesting practices that stood out to him. These ranged from the unique product displays inside shops that attracted customers, an effective sales pitch by a salesman, an objection by a dealer that was effectively handled by the salesperson, a customer's feedback and even interesting things like local food, customs, dresses and monuments from the regions he visited.

Once a month, he would invite the video editor to the office, along with two VCRs. Together, they would transfer the clips Neel had captured onto a VHS cassette. Between the clips, Neel would face the camera and provide the context, and with the editor's help, they created a thirty-minute story that tied the disparate clips into a single central theme for the month. Neel would then ask the video editor to make twenty-five copies of the tape for him.

Next, Neel created an instruction sheet for the person who was going to play the video to his team. The sheet would have instructions. For example, pause the video at 00:14:23 and ask the audience, 'What do you think of the display you saw just now? Do you think it'll help grow sales?' or 'If you were the salesperson in this situation, would you have handled this objection from the dealer differently?'

All twenty-five sales teams in the firm met at their respective local offices in the last week of the month to review the previous month and discuss fresh directions and inputs for the next. Neel would dispatch a copy of the month's video cassette and the instruction sheet to every office, ask each team manager to locally hire a TV and a VCR for the day of the meeting and set aside an hour to play the video in the team's presence. The instruction sheet specified where to pause and the suggested questions to ask the team.

This was Neel's answer to discovering, sharing and codifying best practices across all parts of the country. He aimed to standardise the training process and make it exciting by using the latest technology available.

Have you ever used a new technology or form factor to re-energise a tired process? Do you see an opportunity around you to revive something in which people are losing interest?

_____
_____
_____
_____
_____
_____

Around the same time, Neel's readings exposed him to 'Total Quality Management'—essentially America's answer to Japan's ability to produce high-quality goods at competi-

WHAT WILL YOU DO?

tive prices. Though originally designed for cross-functional process improvement, Neel felt that he could take a few leaves from the book and create impactful training material for the sales function.

Neel started the process by announcing that, from now on, every decision would place the customer at the centre. Every salesperson was asked to identify and report processes that were getting in the way of serving the customer effectively and required an overhaul. Drop boxes, set up in prominent locations in the office, acted as a reminder for people to share their suggestions for improvement. Neel acknowledged every suggestion, and where appropriate, he added feedback. The high point of the initiative was that every time a process change activity was completed, the person who proposed it received a certificate of appreciation, recognising their contribution. The momentum built slowly, but as the certificates started to arrive, the flow of new suggestions picked up.

Next, they prepared the course material for TQM immersion and identified three to four articulate mid-level managers in each region to train everyone on the subject. The hand-picked managers spent a few days at the head office getting trained and practising how they would deliver the material in a classroom setting. They were sent back to the region to roll out the programme only once Neel was satisfied with their readiness.

Japanese words like 'kaizen' (improvement), 'kanban' (signboard), 'muda' (waste), 'poka-yoke' (error proof) and 'gemba' (the real place) soon became a part of the sales lexicon, and examples of these concepts started appearing in the clips that Neel captured for the monthly video magazine. The depth and relevance of the process improvement suggestions from the field also changed dramatically after the training programme was rolled out.

In one of the subsequent video magazines, when Neel went about asking team members to describe in one word how they felt today, words like 'refreshed', 'knowledgeable', 'empowered', 'capable', 'upgraded', 'renewed' and 'competent' could be heard. Sales began to rise across regions, and employee attrition dropped sharply.

Word of how technology was being used to transform the mundane chore of training into something engaging and exciting began to spread. A national business magazine carried a three-page article on TQM and the unique use of a video magazine to standardise training, complete with a colour photograph of Neel. That was a big achievement for a thirty-three-year-old.

WHAT WILL YOU DO?

Is there an opportunity in your work to create a programme by adapting an already established, globally acclaimed process?

_____
_____
_____
_____
_____
_____
_____
_____

The 1990s had arrived, a time when the country had started opening to rest of the world, and reputed international brands were steadily setting up shop here. By now, Neel, who had already spent four years in three roles in this firm and a decade in seven different positions, was welcoming change. Once again, he began entertaining calls from headhunters. He felt that his next stop, while still in operations, should be with a global firm in a category whose challenges were even more complex.

A headhunter friend he met suggested that he connect with some clients who were looking for a business head with an entrepreneurial mind. Neel wasn't entirely sure what that meant—he was seeking employment and not ownership. But he agreed to learn more.

This firm dealt in an even faster moving consumer product compared to the two that Neel had managed in the past, and their business model was unique. All their operations, from manufacturing to distribution, were managed by external partners instead of internally. These partners invested millions of dollars in plants, machinery and other infrastructure, hired thousands of people and were led by a CEO and a complete leadership team of their own. As a result, they were significantly larger than any such partners Neel had worked with before. Neel's firm, as the principal, would authorise the partner to manufacture and sell its product according to defined processes and quality standards. The company also had subject matter experts (SMEs) who would guide the partners in their respective areas.

Neel's role was that of a business manager. He was expected to develop business plans for associated partners, ensure they invested as per plan and monitor that operations aligned with the principal's expectations. The principal aimed to achieve its national business plan through multiple such partners, business managers and a handful of SMEs. This is how they had operated across the globe for almost a century, and now they were here.

However, the role would present challenges far greater than Neel had encountered so far. The fully outsourced nature of operations, the low price point of this firm's products, the impulse-driven nature of the category and

WHAT WILL YOU DO?

the high seasonality leading to infrastructure investments lying under-utilised for most of the year, made it difficult to generate a fair return.

The more Neel thought about the business model, the more it intrigued him. He did not see any reason for the firm to outsource the entire value chain in the hands of a partner. However, he saw the role that was offered to him as a natural next step in his career, an opportunity to gain a completely different experience. He decided to join them.

A month later, just a day before his official start date, Neel received a call from one of the specialists at the firm. The caller was scheduled to meet with one of Neel's assigned partners the next morning and convince him to invest in a particular machinery. He wanted Neel to accompany him. Neel was stunned and he laughed aloud. The industry was new; he had no clue about their manufacturing process, investments or returns, and here he was being asked to meet the partner without even an induction into the business. 'So?' the specialist said. 'What's a better, more hands-on induction than this? Were you expecting a classroom and a whiteboard?'

Neel got a flavour of how this firm operated, and in no time, he became one of them. For the next five years, he embraced their culture and loved every moment. The roller coaster went up and down many times a day, every day. And if there was a place that could teach someone to live with ambiguity and uncertainty, it was this.

Take, for instance, the presentation of the annual business plan, which business managers created for their partners. It was a day-long ceremonial affair that everyone looked forward to. The partner and the CEO of Neel's firm sat at the head of the table. The principal's leadership team and that of the partner were also present. The business manager's key responsibility before the meeting was to align the partner on the investments they would make during the year and the turnover they would commit to. That done, the presentation ceremony was a ritual everyone went through. Neel, however, was either not aware of this nuance or missed it when he was told about it.

Three months into the job, he walked into his first business plan presentation armed with a presentation deck. He had leveraged his knowledge of the industry and the markets, which he had gathered in this period, to create the plan. As soon as Neel was done presenting the deck, the CEO turned towards the partner and, as was the custom, asked if he was committed to the plan. To which the partner said, 'Well, Neel has made this plan. We will go back and study it and get back with our comments on it.' At that moment, it was clear to everyone in the room that Neel had committed the blunder of not aligning the partner beforehand. As people left the room in silence, no one looked at Neel. In that moment, it felt that his career at the firm was over. The CEO walked out too without saying a word, and Neel was left alone in the room.

WHAT WILL YOU DO?

Dejected, Neel looked towards another business manager colleague who was still in the room with eyes that silently said, 'I need help, will you tell me what I should do now?'

Sensing Neel's plight, the colleague walked up to him, held his hand and said, 'Come, let's grab a drink.'

Over the course of the evening, his colleague—already a veteran with three years at the firm—shared the unwritten rules that guided the principal–partner relations, the steps Neel should follow to cement his reputation at the firm and how to strengthen his relations with the partner. He felt that Neel had it in him. But the place was a jungle where no one taught you to hunt. Only those who learnt survived.

Have you faced a similar situation where no one told you what to do, and when you goofed up, everyone washed their hands of you? Did you complain and leave, or did you find a way to learn, made amends and bounced back?

_____
_____
_____
_____
_____
_____
_____
_____

In the following days, Neel met both his CEO and the partner and promised to put together another plan in which he would align both sides at every step of its development. While those around him were uncertain of the outcome and his future at the firm—they'd seen similar disasters unfold before—Neel was clear that he could create a plan in a language that everyone understood and subscribed to.

By this time, Microsoft Excel had been introduced and working with larger data sets had become easier. Neel pulled out as much past data as he could from the files and spent nights feeding it into Excel worksheets. This helped him identify five factors that he found a direct correlation with turnover: plant and machinery, servicing infrastructure, manpower, advertising spends and in-store availability. Neel called these factors the 'Building Blocks'.

The correlations were based on empirical evidence, and that made it difficult for anyone to deny their efficacy. Consequently, it became easy for Neel to align every one of the partner's leadership teams on these building blocks.

Next, Neel engaged with people across the partner's organisation to understand their turnover ambition for the forthcoming year. Using their inputs, he built a consensus target.

From there, Neel calculated how much investment each building block would need to achieve the desired turnover. Since it was a direct extrapolation based on historical patterns, it was not subjective. He also made sensitivity

WHAT WILL YOU DO?

models for each component and projected the drop or rise in turnover because of a 10 per cent increase or decrease in the investment on each building block.

The annual plan meeting was called again. This time, it lasted just about an hour, and when it came to the cardinal question that Neel's CEO asked at the end, all that the partner could say was, 'We will invest every dollar that Neel is asking us to invest and if the outcome turns out as is projected by the plan, and there is no reason that it shouldn't, I will deposit a personal cheque for a million dollars in Neel's account.' Everyone laughed, but it meant a lot to Neel because he felt resurrected. It was too early in the day to step out for a celebratory drink, so the teams returned to their respective workplaces.

That year, two of the three partners that Neel managed were felicitated at a global meet, and in the following year, the 'Building Blocks' model was adopted by most business managers in the country, in full or at least in part.

By now have you started seeing a pattern in how Neel doesn't get discouraged by an adverse situation? Instead, he looks for an alternative that others would consider unconventional, hence not doable. He pivots. Do you see an opportunity to pivot in a sticky situation that you could be facing at home or at work?

_____
_____
_____
_____
_____
_____
_____

In the principal–partner relationship, brand ownership remained with the principal, along with the responsibility of sustaining brand salience and driving consumer desire. While the central marketing teams produced thematic campaigns time to time, and they ran on TV, billboards and print, the task of creating 'arms and legs' for these campaigns in the marketplace fell on the business manager.

By now, Neel had a fair idea of what appealed to customers and excited the trade, and he would personally brief the advertising agency for the local legs of each campaign. The campaigns were well-received by the audience and gave consumption a boost. The local teams were so excited

WHAT WILL YOU DO?

with the results that they went ahead and extended these campaigns beyond their scheduled dates and target groups, resulting in a slight overrun of expenses. However, the central marketing team looked the other way as the bang for the bucks spent was very high.

More than half of the market was consuming Neel's brands because of the operating excellence of the partner that leveraged the salience created by the principal, a perfect collaboration to say the least. Their competitor, also a global player, was doing relatively poorly in the areas managed by Neel's partners in comparison with other geographies.

This is when Neel was offered a position in the marketing team to manage 'marketing execution'. He had already spent four years managing operations with three large partners—the longest he had held on to a single role in his fourteen-year career. He accepted the move, and that year, he did help put some wheels under a couple of large countrywide campaigns.

Five years had flown by, and two roles later, the excitement began to wear off once again. Neel wanted a change, but his condition of not working in two firms within the same industry came in the way of exploring newer opportunities. His headhunter friends would often complain that there weren't too many product categories in the consumer space for him to choose from. They cited examples from professions like banking, advertising and law, where people worked in every firm within the industry before they retired. 'So?' Neel asked. 'Do you expect me to jump across to someone who's been my competitor and help them work on destroying what I have helped build earlier?'

What is your take on working for two firms in the same industry? Would you do it? If not, why not?

_____
_____
_____
_____
_____
_____
_____

Around this time, something new started to brew in the industry. Service businesses, which were hitherto a monopoly of the public sector, were one by one coming into being, from the government to the private sector. In this shifting landscape, Neel saw an opportunity for him to experience another industry. Above all, this was his window to gain the much-desired exposure to the services sector—one that was expected to outstrip physical goods according to every report Neel read.

Neel was approached by a retailing firm which had been taking baby steps for a few years and, despite its relatively low scale, had built a formidable reputation as a much-admired pioneer in that space. They wanted to shift gears by rapidly expanding the business they already had and had plans of branching out into a couple of ancillary businesses, too.

Neel liked what they had built so far and found their plans exciting. However, whoever he spoke to disapproved of his leaving a global firm to join an untested small setup. 'Why would you want to put a well-nurtured career at risk by moving to an upstart? They are so tiny compared to what you're used to. What if they have a change of mind and plans?' they questioned.

Neel responded, 'So? Even the largest of global firms started somewhere in a shack. This, too, could be a global firm someday.'

He switched companies and, in the process, cities. For his previous two moves, Neel had ensured that the next employer's product had greater reach, higher complexity of operation and a larger growth opportunity. These ingredients were necessary to challenge his abilities, and they, in turn, would help grow his capabilities.

Even though the scale of the new firm was much smaller than whatever Neel had managed so far, the ability to do hands-on work and see instant results that this business offered was invigorating. All they needed next was scale—enough to make it complex, so that management would be compelled to step in and simplify it. That, in turn, would make the daily grind enjoyable.

Things didn't unfold as envisaged. Three other businesses, still in the conceptual stage, had to be shelved prematurely. For reasons best known to them, the investors seemed less forthcoming than the expansion opportunities available, and at the end of eighteen months, Neel was left staring at only small growth for the main business, far short of the multiplier they had expected.

With no larger portfolio to manage, the firm did not have room to justify Neel's position or his salary, set in anticipation of a much bigger role and higher turnover. A quick conversation conveyed: 'There were certain expectations we had when we brought you in. However, they did not come true. Hence, it is best that we part company. Take your time, maybe even two or three months, and try and find a new role for yourself.'

These words concluded the meeting. And since it was the time of the year when increments were handed out, Neel was handed his letter, too, but without an increment, since he was being fired, albeit politely.

Neel left the room, mulling over what had just transpired. He wasn't sure whether his forced exit was due to the firm's plans that had not come true, or whether it was he who had not met the management's expectations of him. Net-net, he had just lost his job, and he only had a couple of months to land himself another.

WHAT WILL YOU DO?

Have you ever been fired or had your role made redundant? What was your first reaction? Did you blame other people, yourself, the situation or all of the above sequentially?

_____
_____
_____
_____
_____
_____
_____

Neel did not even have a resume; he had never made one because he never had to look for a change. He had always been headhunted. Instead of bad-mouthing anyone or cursing his fate, Neel took the outcome in his stride and on the same evening started calling his headhunter friends.

The dotcom boom was at its peak, and everyone he called suggested a couple of options. Having seen a few similar fads in the past, Neel wasn't keen on jumping on the trend. He wasn't sceptical about the disruption caused by the dotcom ventures; however, his experience had told him that only a couple of firms with strong fundamentals succeeded in capitalising on these disruptions, while many that were just riding on the wave failed. The private equity firms that bet on multiple ventures simultaneously needed only one venture to succeed for them to get a return. In contrast, the employees who invested their time and were seeking a return on effort could bet on only one option at a time. If that failed, their entire effort could come to nought.

While interviewing candidates in the past, Neel had studied many resumes that went down the slippery slope thanks to one wrong move during a similar boom. Most such people he had met had eventually become rolling stones, switching from job to another, every year, without getting a second chance to enjoy a stable career or a growth path ever again. After this debacle, he already feared meeting the same fate. Hence, he was averse to topping his current mess with another risky entry into an untested sector. Moreover, by now, Neel wasn't alone and had a family, hence the need to land on his feet quickly and on firm ground.

The first six weeks went by without a call from anyone. A reminder didn't help either. At the end of the eighth week, Neel had two leads and both materialised. Neel was grateful that his career had gingerly missed the slippery slide.

WHAT WILL YOU DO?

If you ever lost your job, was your career able to recover from the incident and get back on track? Would you give credit to fate or perseverance, or something else, for the recovery? If it didn't recover or took long, what could have been the reason?

_____
_____
_____
_____
_____
_____
_____

The time came to decide between the two job offers, forcing Neel to take a call. He evaluated the number of functions that the two roles actively interacted with—that was his test of complexity, hence the amount of learning the job had to offer. Based on what he discovered, he went with the offer that promised greater engagement.

It was a pure service business with no physical payoffs for the customer, fulfilling a very basic experiential human need of communicating with others through a recently developed technology that was expected to percolate fast. Since it used natural resources, the sector was highly regulated and under constant scrutiny of the government.

By the time Neel entered, the product had been around for over five years but had not made much headway. The high upfront investment required to offer the service, combined with steep pricing, limited its access only to the rich thus stifling the growth of the category.

The electronics-based, technology-dependent, high capital-intensive category's early employees were those who had been in the computer and photocopying businesses in their past lives. As a result, the industry's pricing and processes mirrored those sectors. Neel wasn't the only one with a consumer marketing background to join the industry at that time. There were a few others with similar expertise who joined Neel's firm and its competitors around the same period.

The entry into this industry of Neel and the likes of him was not met with great enthusiasm by the existing employees. The veterans often scoffed at them, calling the new entrants 'cola and candy boys'. They felt that selling biscuits was different from selling tech-based solutions. In a review meeting, an older colleague challenged Neel and said, 'But this is a tech product, not a packet of chocolate cookies. Customers use different criteria when they buy these.'

'So?' Neel asked. 'Are the people who buy colas, biscuits, washing machines, airline tickets and insurance policies or even open a bank account, different from the ones who use our products? They are the same humans with the same emotional state and financial status. What

WHAT WILL YOU DO?

drives them and their yardsticks for decision-making cannot vary between product categories. Let's pick a few leaves from what the fast-moving consumer goods sector has already done and build a *faster*-moving consumer goods category.'

Similar conversations were taking place in Neel's competitors' offices, too.

In your opinion, do customers use similar criteria while buying a product or a service? Can the principles used for selling biscuits be applied to tech-based products?

_____
_____
_____
_____
_____
_____
_____

Neel started by handling operations for a part of the country, and the new approach brought in by the 'cola and candy boys' started paying off. As a result, the industry expanded more in the six months that followed compared to what it had in the previous five years.

Neel's inputs on pricing, advertising, distribution—shared during meetings and reviews—started getting noticed, even acknowledged. One day, the CEO called and offered him a role at the head office to lead marketing for the country. Neel was overwhelmed and explained that he had been an operations person all his career and knew little about the theoretical concepts often referenced by the marketing professionals. He didn't even know their jargon. He was told, 'So? You seem to know so much more about the customers based on your prolonged and closer exposure to them that you'd be better off running the function based on your intuition rather than by the book.'

Neel moved to the head office as the chief marketing officer; however, he continued to remain connected with the markets and customers. In his first interaction with the advertising agency, he said, 'We know our customers and have a good understanding of their needs. By meeting and talking to them often, we can create more products than we have. I would like to believe that your team has a deep understanding of how we should communicate with our customers. We do not know that art. That's why we have hired you, and we will allow you to do your job without breathing down your necks. As David Ogilvy had once said, "Don't hire a dog and then bark yourself." We will refrain from barking if you exhibit the courage and produce material for us that will make our customers love our products.' The agency folks were surprised because it wasn't often that they heard clients say what Neel just did.

WHAT WILL YOU DO?

Neel stuck with what he had said and refrained from directing art or writing copy, unless it was to throw a challenge when the creative team took longer than it was expected to turn a job around. 'Let me have your inputs, or we will go with what I've just suggested,' he would say when he sent them a dummy creative idea on such occasions. The agency knew that Neel was just egging them on and that he had no intentions of bypassing them. But it did inspire them on for sure, and things worked better and faster instead of being stagnant and slow.

Advertisements across the industry bragged about their superior equipment, of which they had more than anyone else and that their price was the lowest. Neel's only brief to the agency was, 'My customers don't care a hoot about how I do it; they are only concerned with what our service does for them. So, let's talk about that instead of boasting about what we have invested.'

What the agency would come back with was, to say the least, unconventional. It wasn't the kind of advertising that even the adventurous 'cola and candy boys' would have dared to run for their brands.

Should an outsourced agency be allowed to work without close and frequent supervision? Don't regular reviews help avoid delays and aid course correction and wouldn't their absence lead to rework, cost overruns and missed deadlines?

_____
_____
_____
_____
_____
_____
_____

Soon, the firm started gaining recognition for its advertising and how it touched the customers' hearts instead of bragging about its products from rooftops. For three years in a row, Neel's firm and the agency won the campaign of the year award across all industries.

Meanwhile, Neel didn't keep himself busy only producing ad campaigns. He had a very able communications team and he only sat through briefing sessions and gave the final go-ahead to advertising campaigns. More than half his time went into helping guide functions that managed customer touch points. A great ad film can only make the brand look attractive; to acquire and retain a customer, touch points needed to convey the same warmth and a feeling of helpfulness in every human interaction. His operations background of nearly twenty years came in handy on these fronts.

One Monday morning, at the end of the weekly review, his manager announced that Neel would be moving back to operations to head a regional business with complete accountability for the P&L. They had hired another CMO from outside the firm who was already on his way to the office and would be joining by the afternoon. Before the meeting could end, Neel was also advised, 'The region you are taking over had been personally taken to market leadership by me. You have to ensure that the position and profitability of the firm in the region are not destroyed.'

On one hand, Neel felt that this move, and a complete charge of a region, was a reward for the good work that he had done. On the other hand, the secretive appointment of a successor and the hurried announcement made him a bit sceptical about the intent. By now, he had started liking the category so much that he didn't pay much heed to the semantics. He took the change at face value and got down to work.

Should people be told sufficiently in advance before their successors come on board? How should they react in the event they are not informed beforehand?

_____
_____
_____
_____
_____
_____
_____

The next two years were probably the most satisfying of Neel's career. The geography was relatively richer, the team was tightly knit and focused, and the market offered considerable growth potential. Most market leaders with the kind of profitability that Neel's firm enjoyed would have hesitated to experiment with pricing. Not Neel. He boldly introduced low-priced alternatives while maintaining their quality. His careful analysis had told him that their growth would more than offset the losses from cannibalisation, and it did. The region, once expected to stagnate, substantially grew both its top line and bottom line and became the largest and the most profitable region in the country, well ahead of all others.

This success reinforced Neel's belief that it is the market leader's prerogative to make the product more affordable

WHAT WILL YOU DO?

and extend its usage to the next tier of consumers. His experiments had taught him that the best time for a brand to disrupt the market was when the going was good and an external threat was not yet on the horizon. If a weaker competitor initiates a disruption, the leader has no choice but to react—and any reactive move is far less effective than a proactive move. Neel often used the phrase, 'Eat your lunch before someone else does.'

Do you agree that the best time to disrupt is when things are going well? If yes, are there any happy situations in your life that you would like to disrupt before someone else does?

_____
_____
_____
_____
_____
_____
_____

One morning, once again without notice, Neel was asked to return to the CMO position. A potential merger was underway with one of the world's largest global brands, and Neel's experience made him the most suited person to headline the presentations to the potential buyers. He transitioned back to marketing just as he had earlier moved into operations. However, after managing a complete P&L first-hand, he stopped viewing marketing as merely a guardian of the brand and customer touch points. Marketing, he now felt, was responsible for the entire commercial engine that generated revenue for the business. They would do this by pricing strategically to drive optimal acquisition and retention of customers and stimulate usage, and this approach would be tailored across different geographies and customer segments.

So, Neel broke the function into two divisions—communications and commercial—and he made every region replicate this bifurcation for effectively dealing with the head office. The commercial teams created their review mechanisms, which they rigorously followed. Within six months, the firm was realising five percentage points higher revenue per unit sold in a market where hypercompetition had forced price parity amongst competitors.

Meanwhile, the merger presentations prepared by Neel and his colleagues and discussions at the investor level resulted in the sale of the company to a global brand.

The new global team would visit the country often and had initiated the integration plan, which included replacing the local brand with their global one. This was the first time they were proposing to phase out an iconic brand that was one of the most loved in the country. In most of their past acquisitions, the brands hadn't held such stature, and in the handful of cases where they had, the change had taken over a year.

WHAT WILL YOU DO?

Neel was clear that the change, though painful, had to be implemented with precision and speed. It would be like pulling off a Band-Aid in one go so that the duration of the hurt is minimised. He asked his team, who were aligned with his thought process, if they could manage the complete process in ninety days flat, and the team responded affirmatively. They worked backwards from the expected end date, and the brand was changed on the ninetieth day. Such was the effectiveness of the execution that they had to pull back some media spends as the knowledge of brand's transition amongst their customers and non-customers took less than half the time they had had in mind.

Have you ever crashed the timeline of a process by a large factor versus its past delivery? In addition to a detailed plan, were there other factors that helped you deliver? Is there a process whose timeline you could reduce to half or less? How would you go about doing it?

_____
_____
_____
_____
_____
_____
_____

One evening, when Neel was having a drink with one of his expatriate colleagues, the question of who among them would take over as the next CEO came up for discussion. Neel's colleague was clear that, given his commercial and operations experience and a twenty-five-year career spanning across five industries, Neel was the most likely choice and not someone from outside the firm. Neel laughed out loud and said, 'You must be kidding. In terms of designation, money and fame, I have already reached way beyond what I had expected to, or what I thought I was capable of at the time of finishing college. This is the most I could have ever achieved, even in my dreams. I can't even imagine the title of CEO against my name, not in this life.'

This is when Neel was asked to move to the firm's global head office as a marketing director to support the commercial arm of the marketing function. He moved countries this time, and his first task given to him by the global CEO was to discover what differentiates a commercially capable team from one that is not.

WHAT WILL YOU DO?

Have you been offered a position that you had never expected, not even in your dreams? Was your inability to expect it a result of your lower self-worth than what others thought of you, or did you just get lucky? Were you able to live up to the position?

_____

_____

_____

_____

_____

_____

_____

Neel asked for a team of four to help him with his new global assignment, and these individuals were reassigned from their current roles to work with him for a year. The team began by defining what would make an operating company a commercially capable business unit. Based on an objective list of criteria, they identified the six most commercially capable countries from amongst the twenty-two where the firm operated. They then decided to visit each country and understand their practices—listening closely to the local leadership teams and taking copious notes. The fact that the project was a brainchild of the global CEO helped get everyone's attention, including the CEOs of the operating companies they visited.

Armed with notes from six weeks of travel in diverse countries that included New Zealand, Egypt, Germany, etc., the team spent weeks distilling the learnings to ten core capabilities. For each capability, they articulated ten qualifiers that needed to be explicitly displayed for a business to be considered commercially capable.

This list of capabilities and the qualifiers was shared with all countries. They were asked to select which of these qualifiers their business had and which it didn't. This helped identify local, regional and global weaknesses, and work that was needed to eliminate these was initiated objectively. The list of capabilities and their symptoms was so precise and objectively measurable that Neel was tempted to use it as a basis for a book, which he ended up writing, though many years later.

Do you have a methodology for identifying best practices from remote parts of your business and implementing them across its entirety?

_____
_____
_____
_____
_____
_____
_____

This is the time when Neel's father fell ill again, and Neel rushed back home to see him. It wasn't anything serious, but age had taken a toll on him, and its impact was irreversible. The family physician, whom Neel met during the visit, confirmed that he was likely to become even less capable with the passage of time. That evening, during a quiet conversation, his father asked Neel about his earnings, and Neel shared an approximate figure of his annual remuneration. Later that night, he overheard his father ask his mother, 'What does he possibly do for them that they pay him so much? He needs to be careful and shouldn't change his lifestyle; it is unlikely that they'll keep paying him this for long.' Lying in the next room, Neel smiled at his parents' innocence.

It took Neel less than a week to decide to move back to his home country and convey the decision to his manager. There wasn't much room he had left for discussion or negotiation because in his head, Neel was clear that as an only child, he had to be with his father in his final years.

Would you have accorded a higher priority to being with your parent instead of nurturing a global career? Would you have managed the situation any differently?

_____
_____
_____
_____
_____
_____
_____

Around this time, Neel began entertaining exploratory calls from headhunters, and within a couple of weeks, he had two near-closed offers: one from a fast-moving consumer goods company and another from a tech-based aggregator and distributor of content. One of Neel's ex-managers had transitioned from a consumer goods company to a digital service, and Neel called him for advice. The call turned animated quickly; so much so that Neel had to say, 'Why don't you speak into the phone? I can hear you across three continents.'

His advice to Neel was, 'Consumer goods businesses are sequential operations. Each step takes time, so any change would be prolonged. Tech-based services, on the other hand, are complex and demand greater collaboration between functions in real time. Yet in the absence of physical inventory, they allow for quick changes, thus leaving a larger room for experimentation. Having tasted blood with a tech-based service for nine years, you'll be done with your day by lunch if you were to join a consumer goods business again, leaving you bored stiff in six months and wondering what to do with your life.'

Neel accepted the offer from the content delivery firm and joined them as their CEO for his home country after three months.

Part 4

HOW WILL YOU STAY AT THE PEAK FOR LONG?

On his first day as a CEO, Neel felt much the same as he had felt on his first day at school, college and every previous role. Yet there were some notable differences.

He was aware of his anxiety that stemmed from meeting unknown people and dressing to match expectations. However, deeper underlying fears were also at play now. Neel was conscious that people would be secretly assessing his capabilities. He was acutely worried that his limited knowledge about the role and the industry could make him come across as an imposter. He was also certain that at least one, if not more of his direct reports, had hoped to land the role themselves and could be resentful that the position went to an outsider. And that there could be others, too, who would be thinking that someone internal would have made a better fit than this new guy.

A couple of years ago, Neel had undertaken a short course in acting over a few weekends—just for fun. Every time the instructor asked someone to read a script, the students would mimic their favourite actor, rendering the dialogue in a way he or she would have delivered it. After watching a few such auditions, it struck Neel that anyone trying to imitate an established actor can only produce a version that is worse than the original. Moreover, if actors from successive generations had merely copied those who had come before them, then we would have ended up with endless clones of Charlie Chaplin, Humphrey Bogart, Katharine Hepburn and Ingrid Bergman, and we would have never seen the likes of Tom Hanks or Cruise, Robert De Niro, Meryl Streep or Cate Blanchett.

He extended the analogy to the world of business. Although it was likely for anyone stepping into their manager's shoes to behave like them, that temptation needed to be nipped in the bud. Or else, the industry wouldn't grow. It was best to learn from what managers did and didn't, yet respond to the present situation in a way that was unique to an individual and befitted the context.

Do you recall a situation when you were meeting a new set of people with whom you wanted to create a good impression? Were you anxious, and why? How did you cover your anxiety?

HOW WILL YOU STAY AT THE PEAK FOR LONG?

Neel remembered something one of his earlier managers had told him, 'Say something that isn't obvious; otherwise stay quiet.' So, not just on his first day, but for the next few days too, Neel listened more and spoke less. He smiled throughout the day, started many open-ended sentences which he allowed others to complete, and, in the process, learnt about the firm, its challenges, views about the industry and aspirations.

After a week of asking questions and displaying his curiosity, which he skilfully used to mask his ignorance, Neel felt less nervous, more confident and was sure he had sounded much more genuine. He could have taken a different approach: acted like he had the answers, talked endlessly about his past experiences and the great things he had done in his career so far and stated his expectations from the team instead of listening to them—exactly as many former managers had done when they joined the teams he had once been part of. He recalled what he had thought of them, their pompous attitude and how small their boastful words had made him feel. In his twenty-five years of work, Neel had reported to fourteen managers. Maybe three or four of them had taught him what to do. From the others, he had learnt how *not* to lead. He was more grateful to the ones who had inadvertently taught him what to avoid—that learning had shaped his behaviour far more. Neel was determined that his new team didn't think of him the way he had once thought about some of his managers.

Recall your seniors or managers whose behaviour you liked or disliked a lot. What did you learn from them? Did you use these learnings to mould your behaviour?

_____
_____
_____
_____
_____
_____

During his conversations, Neel caught a strong sense of pride amongst the team for their brand, quality and processes. Yet they seemed less confident about how they had leveraged their supremacy in the marketplace. This hesitation had allowed their not-so-great competitors to take pot shots at them and often get away with it. He also sensed a lack of camaraderie amongst his team. They did not crack jokes or take light-hearted digs at each other, not even after the veil of formality had lifted between them and Neel. He decided to probe more into these signs in the coming days.

Eager to take a deep dive into the situation, Neel met his direct reports one on one to understand the issues each individual was facing. The functions he had worked in over the last twenty-five years and the ones he had interacted with closely in his previous roles were easy to grasp. He

HOW WILL YOU STAY AT THE PEAK FOR LONG?

asked them a few insightful questions and offered suggestions that hadn't occurred to the teams, and he could see their faces light up because of his well-informed input.

In contrast, when the discussions moved to functions that he hadn't dealt with before, especially those involving technologies and processes that were unique to this business, he stuck to asking about what he did not understand and avoided making suggestions. His closing remark to the specialists was, 'You know more than me about what you do, and that will always be the case. Hence, do not expect me to tell you how to do what you do, because that is a black box for me. However, I'll keep coming to you with what goes *into* that black box and what I expect to come out of it, leaving you to figure out what needs to happen inside to create the desired outcome for our customers.'

It took a week for Neel to conclude that it would require a few bold actions, some time and lots of money before the business could be taken back to leadership and profitability. Though he did not have a detailed plan, he had a fair idea of the general direction he needed to steer the organisation towards.

Neel asked his direct reports to identify a few of their junior team members who had been around for a long time and were expressive communicators. His assistant set up in-person and telephonic meetings between Neel and these individuals over the next five days. Every day, Neel would speak with eight to ten young colleagues for fifteen to twenty minutes each to get their views on what was working for the firm, what wasn't and their thoughts on what could be done better. This further helped crystallise his views on potential improvements and how prepared the organisation was for taking up the task.

The exercise sent out a positive message in the company that said, 'Hey, the new CEO listens.'

That done, Neel got down to building the business.

He knew that to keep the lights on, he had to do what every successful business does. Top line targets had to be met, which meant acquiring new customers and increasing usage among their existing ones. They had to keep costs under control so the profits could increase. This had to be done consistently: every day, week, month, quarter and year. Neel found this boring, but he knew that this was step one and had to be done.

To get things moving, Neel did what any strategy textbook would say. He identified the loss-making products and markets and exited them. Someone associated with long-standing ties to the business could not have done that for emotional reasons, but Neel didn't hesitate. In markets where they were losing share, he cut prices to match their competitors and quickly regained lost ground. Competitors who had been willing to lose money to gain share began to raise prices after they started losing both share and money. Neel followed suit.

HOW WILL YOU STAY AT THE PEAK FOR LONG?

That done, Neel was certain that he didn't want price cuts to become a habit in the pursuit of market share. For him, share gain should be an outcome of a better product and processes. He remembered his professor at business school who would say, 'The only purpose of a business is to make money. So all a business must do is to buy or make things cheaply and sell them more expensively, and keep improving their efficiencies to increase the gap between their costs and recoveries. Anyone who doesn't do this every day, perishes.'

Neel asked teams to calculate the true cost of manufacturing each product: raw material, manufacturing, capital and other inputs all included. To that, he added the return that was expected by the investors to arrive at the comprehensive unit cost. He was sure that, given the scale and the efficiency of their processes, no competitor could produce their product at a lower unit cost. That became the rock-bottom price—the absolute minimum anyone was allowed to sell at, that too only while countering an aggressive competitor. 'If a competitor is selling below our rock-bottom unit cost, we should encourage our loss-making customers, if we have any, to buy our competitor's products and accelerate our worthy competitor's journey towards bankruptcy.', he would say to those who cited a discount available in the market while asking for one.

After a few public repetitions of the unit cost mantra, it became deeply ingrained across levels and functions. Salespeople, when reporting a competitor's price drop, would often conclude their report with something like '...*however, we should not match their price as it is below our unit price. We should allow them to bleed instead of bleeding ourselves.*' To Neel, the fact that the sales team were no longer asking to match their competitors' prices was an encouraging sign of the organisation's maturity.

Neel also identified that service was the only sustainable competitive advantage and couldn't be replicated in a hurry by competitors. He raised a motto—'Fail less, recover fast'—and this translated to quality and service recovery metrics, which they monitored regularly and pushed towards desired levels, one step at a time.

Several initiatives like these helped boost their top line, reduce costs and improve their reputation. Soon, they were back to being the category leader, and the gap between themselves and their competitors was increasing with every passing quarter. They reported their first profitable quarter one year after Neel had joined.

HOW WILL YOU STAY AT THE PEAK FOR LONG?

When someone achieves the turnaround that they had planned, should they move on, look for more growth opportunities within or seek other opportunities outside the firm?

_____
_____
_____
_____
_____
_____
_____
_____

Neel was happy with what they had achieved in the short run, and so was the team, who looked up to him as a saviour who had led them towards profitability and shielded them from the wrath of their investors. Yet Neel was restless. For the business to survive and thrive in the long run, the organisation had to sense and respond to changing technologies, regulations, customer habits, economic conditions and competitive intensity which were outside the scope of their influence. They had to become resilient to the external environment, over which they had no control. Neel took it upon himself to help the firm get there. His every action from that day on was aimed at achieving this goal.

Neel would often tell the story of a cigarette lighter brand struggling with declining sales. At first, they wondered if it was because people were smoking less than they did before. However, rising cigarette sales nullified that hypothesis. It took the company many years and a new management to realise that most lighters were not bought but gifted. Eventually, the social stigma around smoking caused people to start gifting pens instead of lighters. The company believed it was in the cigarette lighter business, but in reality, it was in the business of products that were gifted.

After sharing that story, Neel would ask the room, 'What business are we in?' He would conclude by pointing out that companies often fixate on the form factor of what they sell, rather than the underlying customer need they fulfil—just as the makers of radios, LP records, cassette tapes and CDs all thought that they were in the business of selling products, when in fact, they were all delivering a musical experience, till their respective technologies became obsolete.

This exercise helped align teams around a shared understanding of the core customer need that their products fulfiled. It made everyone vigilant, encouraging conversations about changes in customer expectations and emerging technologies that could serve the same need differently.

HOW WILL YOU STAY AT THE PEAK FOR LONG?

What is the core customer need that your business or any other business you know of serves? Can a competitor with access to a new technology serve the same need better than you or at a lower price?

_____
_____
_____
_____
_____
_____
_____
_____

Neel's obsession with people and their behaviour, something which had started during his time in business school, began to resurface. With the opening of the economy and progress of globalisation, everyone had access to capital, technology and customers, and the availability or absence of these factors could no longer make or destroy a firm. In his opinion, it was people who determined the rise as well as the fall of an organisation. Hence, the knowledge base they possessed, how empowered they were to use that knowledge to eliminate what didn't work and replace it with what did, would define a firm's future success. 'People are the new corporate muscle,' he would say often.

Neel realised that resistance to change and unwillingness to think beyond what was apparent were most prominent amongst those who had spent their entire careers in a single industry—like most of their employees. Even those who had switched jobs had typically done so within the same industry. Despite being highly committed and hard-working, they were prone to rejecting most new ideas by saying that they had been tried before and hadn't worked. No radical suggestions came from this lot either.

So, Neel announced a change in their hiring policies: all future employees, unless they were required for domains that needed deep industry expertise, would now be sourced from outside their industry. They never deviated from this rule, and within a few years, most positions across levels were filled by talent who brought a fresh perspective, were open to experimenting with ideas that had worked in the industries they came from and viewed customers more broadly—not just as *their* customers.

Life had taught Neel that circumstances are often beyond our control, but our actions can be within. People who let hurdles overwhelm them were less likely to have a plan in the event of failure, when compared with those who took adversities in their stride without letting them impact their ability to plan and execute an effective response. Hence, when it came to choosing people, Neel focused more on their attitude rather than their skills. If two individuals with an identical skill set were available, he went for the one who smiled more often.

Neel had his own way of identifying the positive thinkers. When a candidate came to meet with him, he would casually ask how the journey was and whether it was easy to find their office. Candidates who complained about the traffic, heat, rain or any other hurdle they had encountered along the way had some ground to cover if they hoped to earn Neel's approval. The ones who had taken the hurdles in their stride, and better yet, shared an interesting incident or a valuable learning from the hardships they faced, usually landed the job if their skills matched the role.

What should one look for while hiring, attitude or aptitude?

_____
_____
_____
_____
_____
_____
_____

Neel believed that the speed with which an organisation responded to change was dependent on how many layers a decision had to pass through before its execution could be initiated. He prompted people to question the role of each organisational level and to look for any two successive layers of humans who merely supervised each other without adding real value. They found two such levels—totalling four layers—two of which seemed redundant.

When challenged, the teams argued, 'One person can only manage five or six people. Layers are necessary to break the span.'

Neel said, 'Why can't twelve, even fifteen people, report to one manager? Does a manager have to meet every one of his subordinates every day? An increased span gives our people more space, prevents managers from constantly breathing down their necks and allows them to work in peace.

'Moreover, with the advancement in data sciences, dashboards now provide real-time information and alert managers when something deviates from expectations. These alerts can help managers focus on team members who need support, while leaving those performing well to continue without unnecessary interference, at least in the short term.'

Neel suggested removing two of these four overlapping layers and increasing the span of control to fifteen. The initial response of the impacted teams was far from positive. They viewed it as a cost-cutting effort on the part of the management that would overburden those who remained. Neel reassured the teams that not one individual would be asked to go. Instead, the transition to the new structure with fewer layers would happen gradually, over two years or even longer, by simply not back-filling roles lost to attrition. Whenever someone left or was promoted, his or her role would be merged with another person's, slowly increasing people's spans. In less than two years, almost everyone had larger and meatier roles, and any decision had to cross only four levels that now remained between the customer-facing employee and Neel.

However, fewer layers came with reduced promotion opportunities as there were now fewer rungs on the ladder. This, in turn, sparked a new idea in Neel's mind. He recalled that in his career, a promotion or an increment had always made him happy, yet that high lasted a few days or at best weeks. The moments of joy he remembered vividly, even after decades, were the ones when his manager expanded his span of control or added another role to his portfolio. For Neel, those moments signalled trust and recognition—he was exceeding his manager's expectations and was seen as an employee capable of handling more. Taking a leaf from this, he suggested a new approach to the leadership team: in the event of a resignation, they should first look internally for someone ready to absorb the departing person's responsibilities in addition to their own. Only if no suitable internal candidate was found should the role be filled externally. Neel felt that this would foster a team with very high self-esteem, where people felt confident of opportunities coming their way from within the organisation, not just from outside. This would retain and attract those who were not obsessed with levels and promotions and were genuinely excited by meaningful work and increasing responsibilities.

What are the advantages and pitfalls for a firm to be the first to create a lean organisation structure with fewer levels and larger spans of control?

_____
_____
_____
_____
_____
_____
_____

The business was growing rapidly, and as a result, everyone's attention was diverted to managing the short term. This came at the cost of the time they had begun investing in looking ahead and preparing for the future. Hiring requests poured in from every function, and more than half the firm was busy managing dashboards while interviewing candidates. Their office space had tripled in four years and was still running short of room. A back-of-the-envelope scribble told Neel that the number of employees would grow another fourfold if their five-year business plan were to materialise. That worried him because he was aiming to beat the five-year plan. Neel had always wanted to build a large business which had the heart of one that was small, and the ballooning headcount and office space seemed to be coming in the way of his plans.

Neel voiced his concern at a leadership meeting, which set everyone thinking about a potential solution. By this point, they were all deeply aligned when it came to the culture of the organisation. In the next meeting, numbers were put forth detailing the levels and functions with the highest hiring growth. A quick eyeballing of the tables showed that nearly all the surge was in roles focused on repetitive execution. In contrast, the count of employees involved in planning, process design or quality checks had not grown nearly as much.

However, everyone in the room agreed that growth required people to make it happen, and if an opportunity knocked, teams had no choice but to expand. They saw it as a happy problem. The HR head, with the help of a consultant, compiled data that showed their employee strength was at par with other firms that had similar turnover or volume of customer transactions.

'So?' Neel said. 'If others are not conscious of their efficiency or culture, we shouldn't either? Are we also saying that in ten years, half the country will be consuming our services, while the other half is busy delivering them? If that were to happen, who would drive the Uber taxis?'

While everyone laughed, a team member suggested reducing the load on people by automating all possible manual processes. The idea quickly gained traction; this transition to using bots would reduce manual errors, cost them less and help slow down the increase in manpower, which was likely to become a bottleneck.

Neel appreciated the thought and added, 'I think that's a great idea, and we do need to propel the pace of automation. How about creating a cross-functional task force to identify the processes that could be handled by bots? I also feel that we need to outsource all our repetitive and non-value-adding tasks to specialist partners who can manage them on our behalf. My wife is a homemaker like my mother was, and she does less than half the household tasks my mother used to do when I was growing up. It gives her more time to grow her small business and ensure the well-being of our children. We've embraced this shift in our homes already; why does it make us uncomfortable to replicate it in the workplace?' One member was concerned that outsourcing could result in them losing control over the processes that were core to their differentiation.

'I'd agree *if* the proposed specialist partners would run these processes however they pleased,' Neal said. 'That's not the idea. We need to design the processes ourselves, create the platforms they'll run on and execute them internally for a while. Only once we are completely satisfied will we hand them over to the partners. Even after that, quality checks must remain with our teams. That way, we ensure standardised execution with no room for deviation. These are repetitive tasks and not creative processes; hence, we can expect such outcomes.'

Everyone was on board after they agreed that the outsourced partners would be made to sign off on service-level agreements and agree to face penalties in the event of deviations. Neel closed the meeting with, 'Let us follow a rule: "Strategy in, ops out." That should give us the time and space that is necessary to keep an eye on the future and respond to its needs.'

Which of the tasks around you would you classify as repetitive? Can these be outsourced to a specialist partner?

_____
_____
_____
_____
_____
_____
_____

During his travels to the regional offices and customer visits, Neel would sense a hunger amongst employees to know more about the initiatives that the company was undertaking, why they were choosing to do the things they did and what the impact of what they had done so far was. He understood that while teams at the head office were aware of everything that was happening, people in the field were largely in the dark. The monthly magazine focused on reporting celebrations and other company events and showed happy employees participating in them. One Saturday morning after breakfast, Neel poured himself a cup of coffee and started writing an email to all employees. He wrote about 200 words on where the company planned to be in a couple of years from now and what would get them there. All his points were expressed in a language that the last person in the hierarchy could understand and relate to. He signed off by seeking suggestions, both on the organisation's proposed destination and the direction that he had visualised in his email.

Neel was overwhelmed by the response. Most had just restated what Neel had said, but that wasn't important. Neel was excited by the eagerness displayed by the teams; to him, the very fact that people chose to write back was a sign of their engagement. From then on, writing to them became his post-breakfast routine every Saturday. He shared updates on what they were doing, asked for ideas on issues that were under deliberation and even forwarded an article or a link to a video that had inspired him during the week. The response rate continued to soar. Colleagues began referencing his emails during field visits, and these became a significant part of their conversations. Neel also noticed that team members discussed his messages among themselves, and his words were beginning to influence how they thought, one idea at a time.

Once a year, the leadership team would prepare a long-term strategy deck for the board that would shape the forthcoming annual budget. This led Neel to suggest that they hold open houses across the country and walk every employee through a simplified summary of the strategy and budget deck. Until then, open houses had largely been celebratory events for awarding the previous year's best performances. Additionally, questions from attendees would centre around salaries, increments and benefits. Neel's idea did not meet with great support; many colleagues felt that the strategy was meant to be confidential, and sharing such sensitive information in an open house made the company susceptible to leaks that would reach their competitors. Others said that frontline employees who were singularly focused on hitting daily targets were unlikely to gain much from their five-year strategy.

Neel disagreed. He said, 'So? Isn't our strategy about growing the industry first, and then growing ourselves as a natural outcome? If the competitors become aware of our plans and replicate our efforts, that only helps us. Besides, I've always believed that people who know *why* they are doing something do it better than those who don't. That was the reason why our parents bought the *Tell Me Why* books for us when we were young. When people know the reason behind their work, they bring heart and mind in addition to their energy. They work purposefully if they know why they are doing what they do.'

Questions at that year's open house were mostly about the company's long-term ambitions. Many attendees added a unique perspective that the leadership team was unfamiliar with, and including that reality in the firm's plans was necessary for prospective strategies to materialise. These valuable inputs would have continued to lie buried under the clamour for pay, promotion and benefits had they not changed the format of the open house.

Do the dangers of opening up the organisation's strategy and action plans to all its people outweigh the benefits?

_____
_____
_____
_____
_____
_____
_____

Neel urged his colleagues to attend relevant international fairs and encouraged them to accept speaking invitations at industry forums. He would visit two to three international industry fairs every year; some of his colleagues accompanied him. Neel would invite experts from sectors like banking, education and other industries whose nature of operations was different from theirs to speak with the senior team, allowing for open Q&A. Exposure to diverse businesses and cultures would open the team's minds to new ideas and boost their progress.

For instance, in one such meeting with a banker friend, the team explained their need for external funding to bridge a couple of years until they turned cash positive, and their difficulty securing bank debt due to a weak balance sheet. After a few questions, the banker realised the funds were intended for imported capital equipment and recommended buyer's credit—an overseas discounting of bills backed with a letter of credit, with payment deferred for two years. That one knowledge-sharing session unlocked a large enough funding source for them till the business started generating cash again.

It took a couple of years to outsource most repetitive functions; however, Neel realised that it wasn't a process that would ever end. Core processes that added value today would eventually become commodities someday, ripe for siphoning. The emergence of specialists for some of these hitherto specialised tasks made it more efficient for an outsourced partner to deliver, while also allowing them to update to the latest technology in real time. The team kept looking for new opportunities for outsourcing.

With operations outsourced and remaining roles merged, the organisation was at its leanest ever. This is when Neel fired the final salvo to build the self-sustaining organisation he had been working on all this time.

He wrote an email to all employees that said:

Dear all,

I write to you today, keeping in mind the complete transparency amongst us that has helped us reach where we are.

It's been a few years since we've been working together to build a self-sustaining organisation that can survive external threats, which we often have no control over.

Some recent unforeseen threats that would have otherwise destabilised us for long were managed in a manner that caused very little disruption to the business. Deep dives to understand how we responded tell us that we need three critical ingredients to successfully handle such threats in the future. These are:

a. A lean organisation with fewer levels
b. Teams that collaborate
c. An empowered frontline

We have done enough in the last few years to trim unnecessary fat and are a lean organisation in which each person is doing more than they would have in the past. Our deliveries did not suffer when people were given additional roles and responsibilities, which demonstrates that we are a responsible crew and are hungry for and capable of managing more.

HOW WILL YOU STAY AT THE PEAK FOR LONG?

We are no longer in an industrial era where people were paid by the hour or for the number of pieces they produced. Businesses have moved from managing pieces to managing knowledge, which doesn't require sitting for eight hours a day, six days a week, in an office or a factory. Knowledge work can be managed from anywhere.

Therefore, I propose we stop marking attendance and let people work from home when it is not necessary to come in. Teams can decide amongst themselves when and how long they need to meet in person. My experience suggests that while whiteboard thinking, which helps make new plans, happens best when everyone is in the same room, reviews of ongoing activities are more efficient online. However, I'd leave the option of when to work from the office and when not, to *your* judgement.

There will remain some roles like sales and service that can only be performed in person and these will require physical presence on all days of the week.

While suggesting a hybrid mode of work, let me state that working from home is not a privilege nor is coming to office a punishment. The months that I spent working from home during the lockdown had me work longer hours than usual. And I did miss coming to working and the animated conversations with my colleagues.

Our business requires collaboration across multiple functions—from process conception through creation and delivery. Misalignment at any stage can result in incomplete delivery. To foster greater collaboration amongst functions, I propose that we dismantle our current office layout, which is currently divided into departments that each have their rooms, cabins and partitions. In its place, let us create open spaces that have no cabins or rooms. No one will have an assigned seat, regardless of their designation or level. People will sit with whosoever they are collaborating with at that moment, and may have to move seats a few times a day. That includes me and the leadership team, too.

To empower our frontline colleagues, I suggest that we deliberate and agree on specific areas where they can take business calls without their manager's approval. Once we have agreed, we can document these for all to know.

We want to take our company to a stage where, in the event of a crisis, our junior teams from across functions can assemble, assess the situation, agree on the solution and get into execution mode without seeking our approvals, while keeping us posted.

Once they have practised doing this for some time, they'll do an even better job in their respective cross-functional project teams.

Let me know what you think.

Best,

Neel

Is dropping conventional norms like attendance, leave, hierarchy-based perks, etc., a wise move? Would it empower people or lead to confusion and inefficiency?

_____
_____
_____
_____
_____
_____
_____

The taste of the cooking is in the eating. All the transformation that Neel inspired, while working against many odds, would have been meaningless if the outcome was no better, or worse, than following the conventional path.

But the course Neel set enabled the team to face every disruption that hit the industry in a way that only strengthened them by a notch or more, every time.

Their business came under the scrutiny of government regulation. A bureaucrat in a brief tenure whimsically altered the industry's pricing mechanism, causing widespread confusion and havoc for customers across all brands. Neel's team quickly rallied, assessed the situation and not only recalibrated their pricing but devised a way to communicate the changes to their customers. This helped them brave the storm that had been unleashed on the industry with the least confusion and pain for their customers. The resulting confidence among their dealers after this episode made them more willing to recommend the brand to their customers.

Then, there was COVID-19. Everyone was ordered to stay indoors. Again, the teams assembled, assessed and planned. In seven days, they were able to get their supply chain together by assembling all available resources, some online, others physical.

While attending an international fair, Neel came across a new technology that was a potential threat to the business—it offered a ready-made disintermediation opportunity for anyone who wanted to snatch their customers. It reminded him of how Nokia users moved to smartphones, and Neel's first response was fear of obsolescence.

But by now, Neel had encountered enough such moments to know that fear didn't serve much purpose. The confidence he had in the team's ability to resurrect itself reassured him, and he asked, 'What is it that someone from outside the industry can do to disrupt us which we can't do ourselves? After all, we understand our customers' needs better than anyone else, and that should give us the right to win in every event. Hence, instead of treating the new tech as a competitor, what if we were to treat it as a friend?'

Sure enough, they were able to articulate how they would leverage the new technology to build an alternate product. Cross-functional teams were briefed on the expected outcome, and they worked in project mode for a year, delivering a product that an external player would have taken twice as long to build. They were the first off the block to harness the disruptive invention and had just bought themselves ten to fifteen years till the next disruption surfaced from the labs.

A few such instances, and the teams soon became experts at sensing signs of disruption. It didn't scare them. On the contrary, they went out of their way to look for ways in which they could disrupt the status quo themselves. They saw it as a stepping stone, one which allowed them to differentiate and grow the business and their reputation. These repeated acts of transformation became a source of inspiration and a powerful way to induct new employees into their way of thinking and working—one that stood apart not just in their industry but across many others.

What are the disruptions that your business could be facing? How do you plan to address them?

_____
_____
_____
_____
_____
_____
_____

The teams no longer waited for problems to surface. They anticipated them early and started working on prevention processes. This approach was easier and less costly when compared to solving roadblocks only after they surfaced as full-blown hurdles.

The teams were now managing the business, and Neel found himself increasingly redundant with each passing day. He had already spent fifteen years in this business and had been working for nearly four decades in his professional career. For someone who was an underconfident and indecisive young boy, he often wondered at what stage of his life he had stopped following the direction of tradition, had started challenging conventions and had learnt to pivot.

Whenever that shift had occurred for him, he was so glad it had. Each time he took a contrarian path and saw its impact—not just on outcomes but on how it made him feel about himself—it increased his confidence. He never looked back.

Now, Neel feels ready to hand over the reins of the business to someone who can take it to the next level. As he reflects on what comes next, he finds himself at a crossroads. Should he take on board positions and share his experience and time to guide other companies on their journeys? Or should he pick a longer lever, teaching and mentoring students and young managers who, in turn, could go on to shape many businesses.

HOW WILL YOU STAY AT THE PEAK FOR LONG?

What do you think Neel should do next?

_____
_____
_____
_____
_____
_____
_____
_____